A
MANUAL OF THE LODGE;

OR,

𝔐onitorial 𝔍nstructions

IN THE DEGREES OF

ENTERED APPRENTICE, FELLOW CRAFT, AND MASTER MASON,

ARRANGED IN ACCORDANCE WITH THE

AMERICAN SYSTEM OF LECTURES:

TO WHICH ARE ADDED

THE CEREMONIES OF THE ORDER OF PAST MASTER RELATING TO INSTALLATIONS, DEDICATIONS, CONSECRATIONS, LAYING OF CORNER-STONES, ETC.

BY

ALBERT G. MACKEY, M.D.,

PAST GENERAL GRAND HIGH-PRIEST OF THE GENERAL GRAND CHAPTER OF THE UNITED STATES,
AUTHOR OF A "LEXICON OF FREEMASONRY," "BOOK OF THE CHAPTER," "THE
RITUALIST," "CRYPTIC MASONRY," "SYMBOLISM OF FREE-
MASONRY," ETC.

A NEW EDITION, REVISED AND ENLARGED BY THE AUTHOR.

"Antiquity considered Initiation as a delivery from a living death of vice, brutality, and misery; and the beginning of a new life of virtue, reason, and happiness."—WARBURTON.

NEW YORK:

EFFINGHAM MAYNARD & CO.,

SUCCESSORS TO

CLARK & MAYNARD, Publishers,

771 BROADWAY AND 67 & 69 NINTH ST.

1891.

TO

WINSLOW LEWIS, M. D.,

PAST GRAND MASTER OF MASSACHUSETTS,

THIS WORK

Is Dedicated,

NOT MORE

AS A TRIBUTE OF THE RESPECT WHICH I FEEL

FOR

HIS INTELLECTUAL ATTAINMENTS,

THAN

As a Token of that Sincere Affection long since won from me,

BY THE

LARGENESS AND KINDNESS OF HIS HEART.

PREFACE.

THE popularity which has been accorded to the "Book of the Chapter" has induced me to believe that a Manual of the Three Symbolic Degrees, prepared according to the same method which had guided me in the composition of that work, would be equally acceptable to the craft.

The present volume has, therefore, been written to supply what I have long supposed to be a desideratum in Masonic literature, namely, the means of enabling the young Mason or the recent initiate more thoroughly to understand the ceremonies through which he has just passed, and to extend his researches into that sublime system of symbolism of which in the ordinary lectures of the Lodge he has received only the faint outlines. Many who anxiously desire to attain "more light" on the obscure subject of Masonic symbolism, and who would, if possible, learn more of the true signification of our emblems and allegories, are either unwilling or unable to devote to these objects the time and labor requisite for poring over the ponderous volumes of Masonic writers in which these subjects are discussed.

To such students, a manual arranged so as to facilitate inquiry, by making every explanation correspond, in order of time and place, with the regular progress of initiation, must be of great value, because its study involves neither a great expenditure of time, which many can not well spare, nor does it demand more intellectual exertion than almost every one is able to bestow.

In obtruding another monitorial instructor on the fraternity, already too much burdened with this class of publications, I can offer only this improved method of teaching as my excuse. I have made no innovations, but have sought to accommodate the order of ceremonies to the system of lectures long since adopted and now generally prevailing in this country.

But these lectures are only the alphabet of Masonry. He who desires to appreciate the whole truth and beauty of Masonic symbolism and philosophy, must go still further and make profounder researches. To enable such an inquirer to accomplish this task, I have written the present work in the humble hope that my labor will not be altogether in vain.

A. G. MACKEY.

April 1st, 1862

CONTENTS.

SYSTEM OF MONITORIAL INSTRUCTION.

PAGE

Opening and Closing the Lodge 11
Forms of Prayer... :5
ENTERED APPRENTICE'S DEGREE............................... 18
    Symbolism of the Degree........................... 18
    First Lecture...................................... 19
First Section 20
    Shock of Entrance................................. 20
    Rite of Circumambulation.......................... 22
    Three Gates of the Temple......................... 26
    Obligation of Secrecy............................. 26
    Unwritten Landmarks..... 27
    Shock of Enlightenment....... 29
    Lambskin Apron.................................... 82
    Northeast Corner.................................. 85
    Working Tools 84
    Archives of the Lodge............................. 36
Second Section.. 87
    Preparation 88
    Belief in God..................................... 40
    Left Side... 40
    Right Hand 40
    Badge of a Mason.................................. 41
    First Instructions................................ 41
    Lesson of Charity..... 41

	PAGE
Third Section	42
Symbolic Extent of the Lodge	44
Mystical Ladder	48
Furniture and Ornaments of a Lodge	49
Three Symbolic Lights	51
Movable and Immovable Jewels	52
The Tabernacle	54
Orientation of Lodges	55
Point within a Circle	56
Three Great Tenets	58
Four Cardinal Virtues	59
Charge	61
FELLOW CRAFT'S DEGREE	64
Symbolism of the Degree	64
Second Lecture	65
First Section	65
Precious Jewels of a Fellow Craft	66
Second Section	67
Operative and Speculative Masonry	68
Pillars of the Porch	69
Symbols of Unity, Peace, and Plenty	71
Orders of Architecture	72
Five Senses of Human Nature	77
Seven Liberal Arts and Sciences	80
Charge	86
Lecture on the Winding Stairs	87
MASTER MASON'S DEGREE	95
Symbolism of the Degree	95
Third Lecture	96
First Section	97
Working Tools	98
Second Section	99
Wayfaring Man	101
Sprig of Acacia	102
Clefts in the Rocks	103
Grand Master's Jewel	103
Five Points of Fellowship	106
Third Section	108
Wisdom, Strength, and Beauty	109
Charge	114

ANCIENT CEREMONIES OF THE ORDER.

PAGE

SECTION I.—Consecration, Dedication, and Constitution of a Lodge 119

    Form of Petition............................ 119

    Preparatory Steps........................... 119

    Form of Dispensation........................ .120

    Warrant of Constitution........ 122

    Consecration........................ 126

    Dedication................................. 132

    Constitution............................... 132

    Installation of the Officers of a New Lodge..... 133

  II.—Annual Installation of the Officers of a Lodge....... 147

  III.—Installation of the Officers of a Grand Lodge........ 158

  " IV.—Ceremony observed at Grand Visitations........... 172

  " V.—Festivals of the Order........................... 174

  " VI.—Ceremony observed at Laying the Foundation Stones

    of Public Structures...... 177

  " VII.—Dedication of Freemasons' Halls................. 187

  " VIII.—Funeral Service 200

  " IX.—Regulations for Processions........... 202

APPENDIXES.

APPENDIX I.—The Twenty-five Landmarks of Freemasonry. 213

  " II.—The Old Charges.. 215

  " III.—The General Regulations.................. 278

ENTERED APPRENTICE.

FIRST AND SECOND SECTIONS.

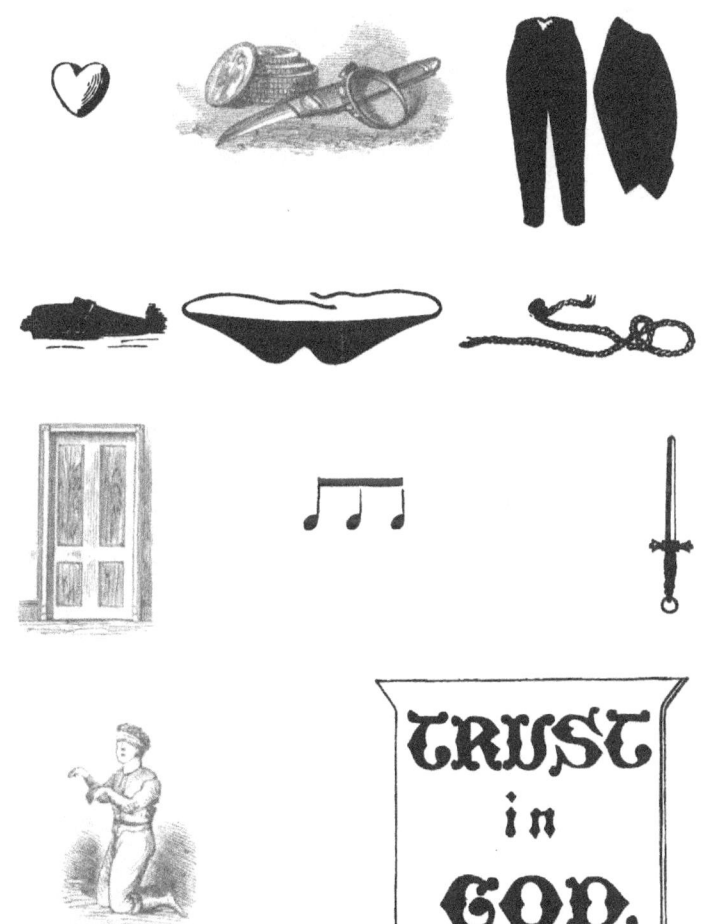

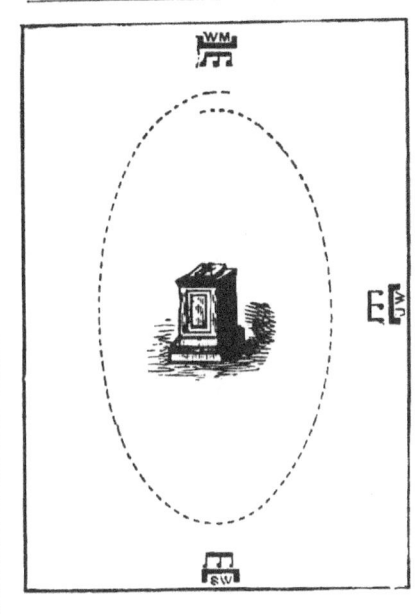

ENTERED APPRENTICE.—THIRD SECTION.

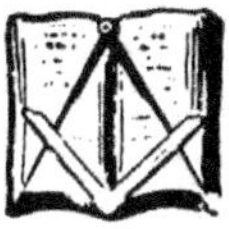

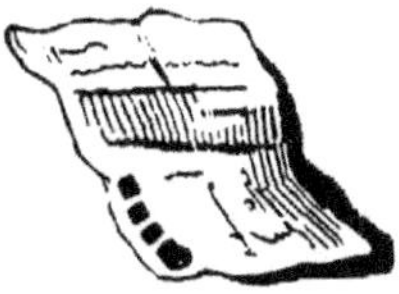

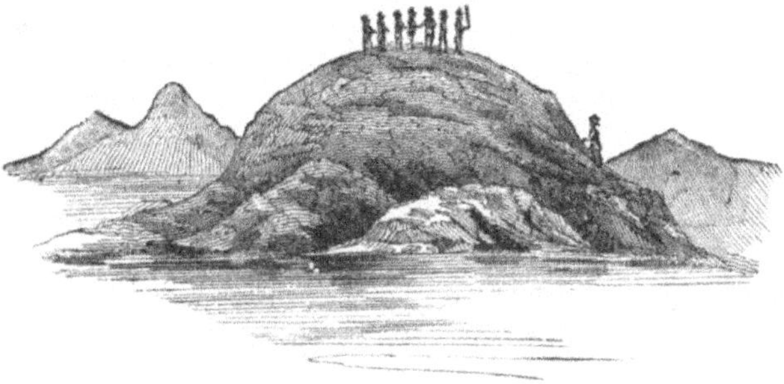

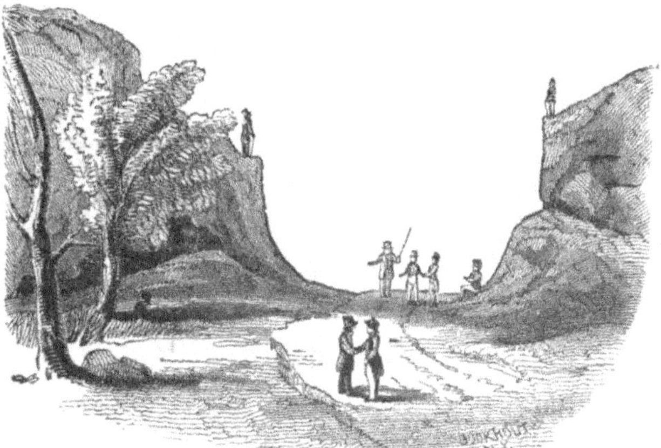

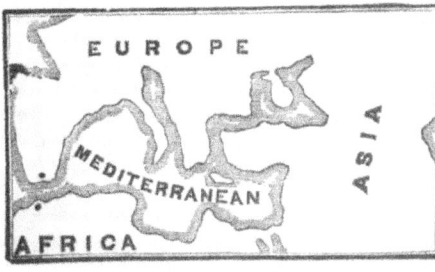

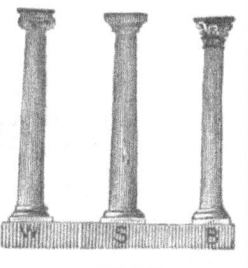

ENTERED APPRENTICE.—THIRD SECTION.

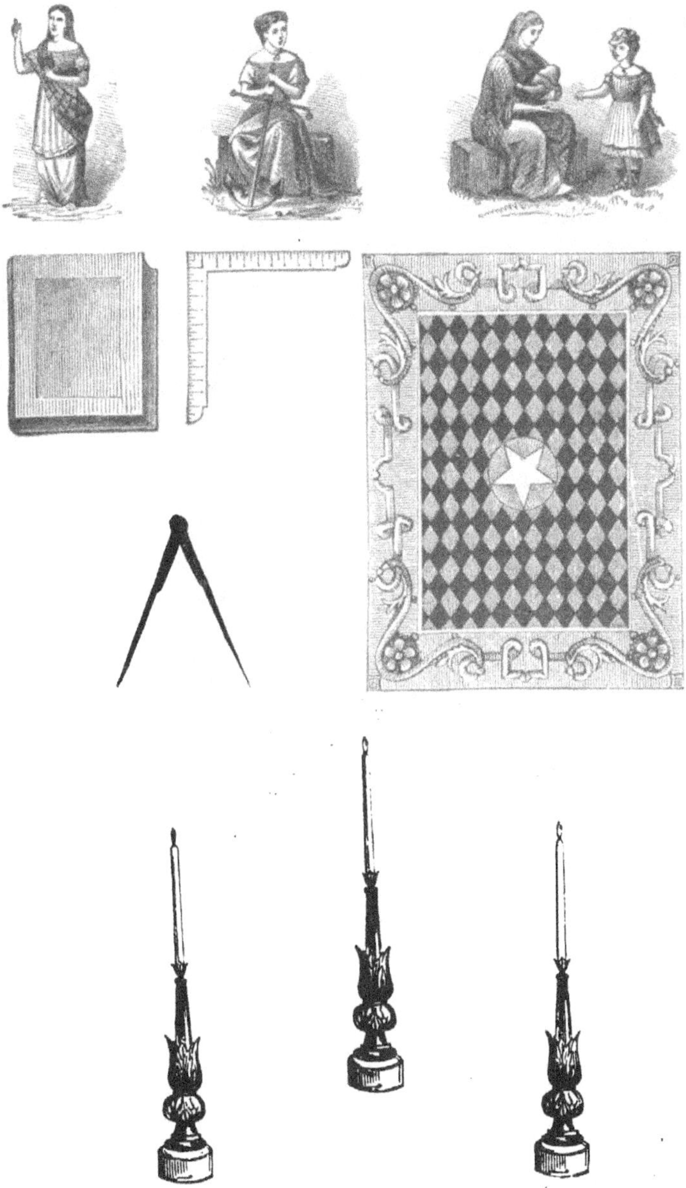

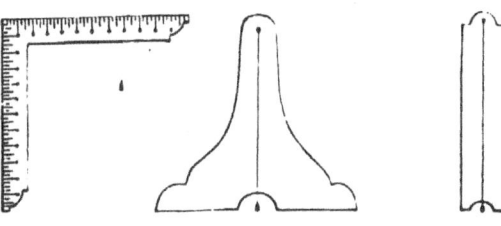

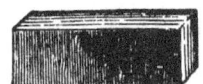

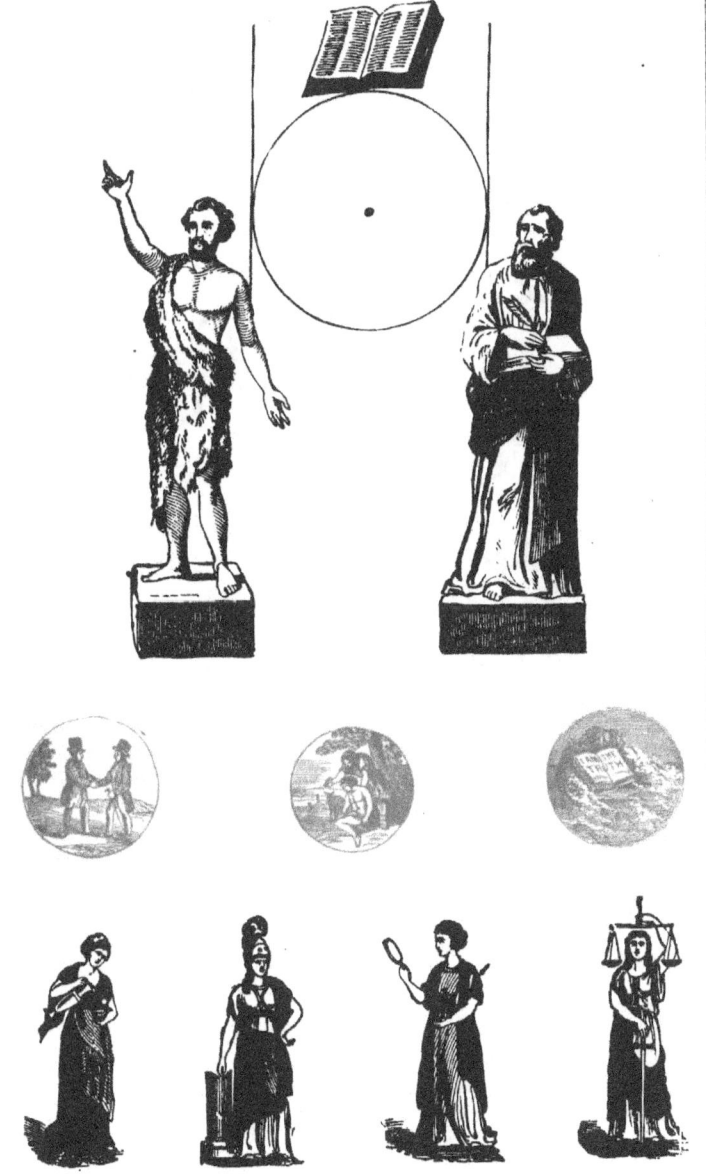

GUTTUR, ... the Throat.

PECTUS, ... the Breast.

MANUS, ... the Hands.

PEDES, ... the Feet.

FELLOW CRAFT.

FIRST SECTION.

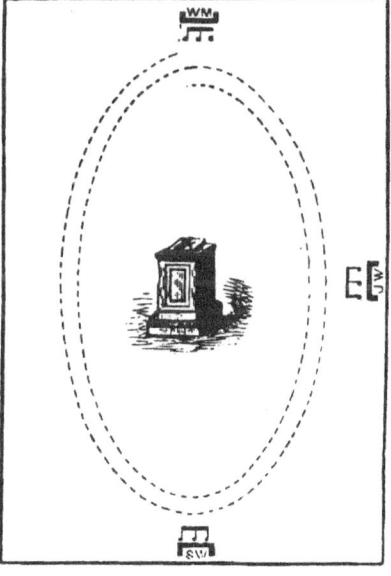

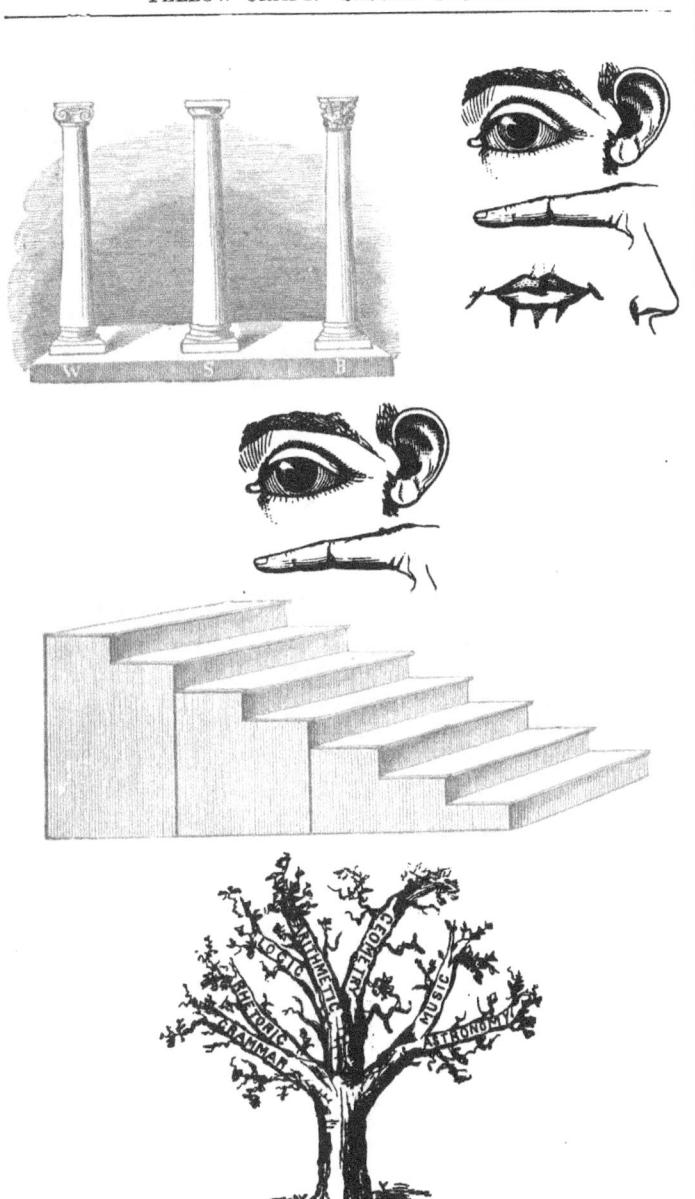

MASTER MASON.

FIRST SECTION.

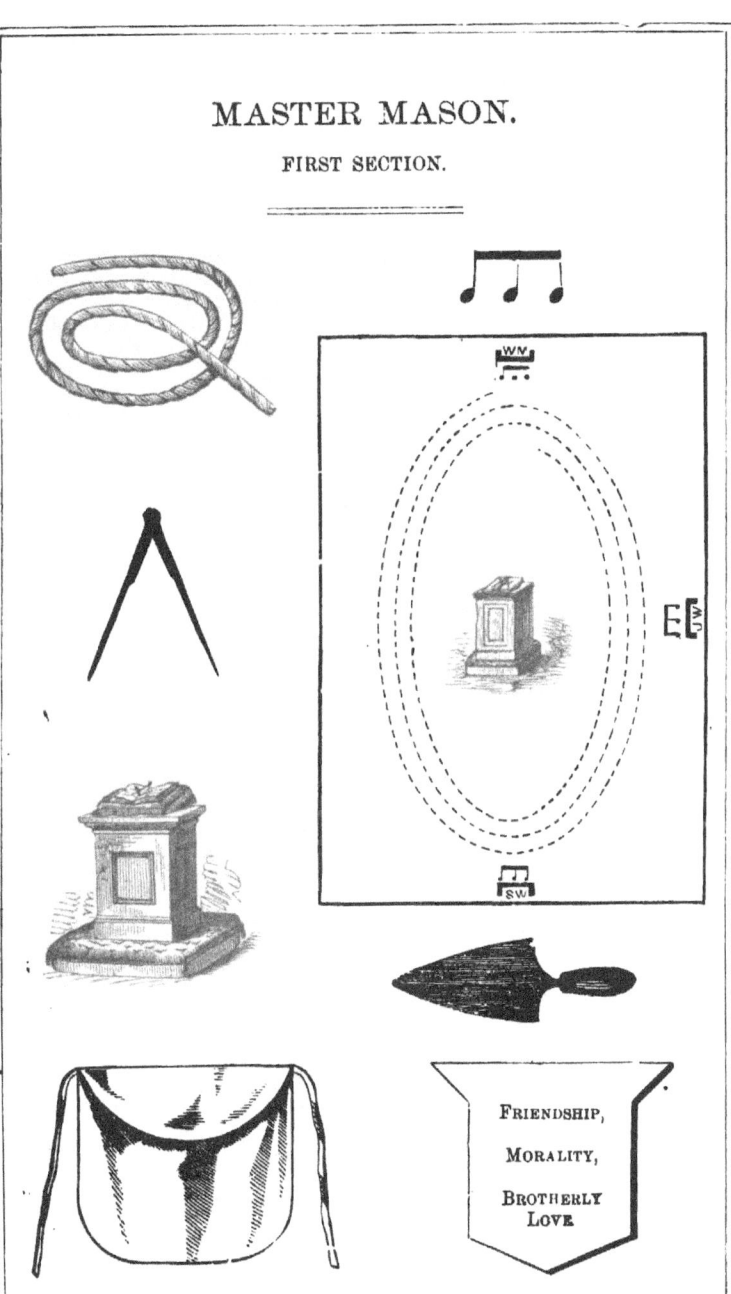

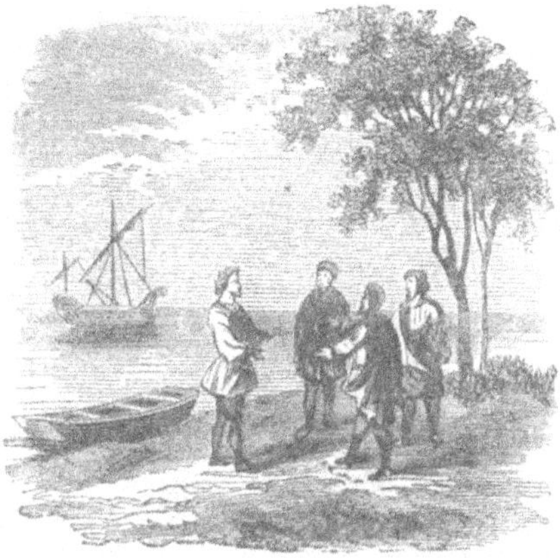

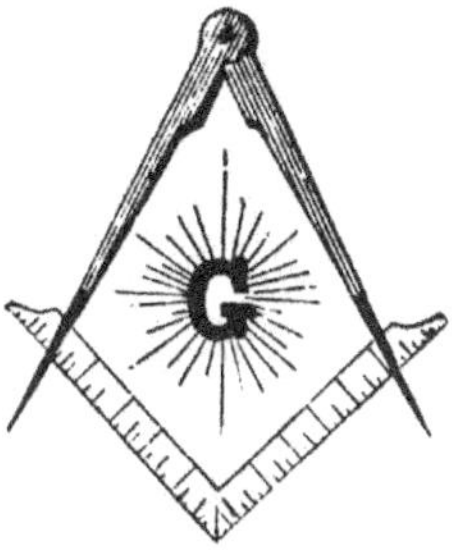

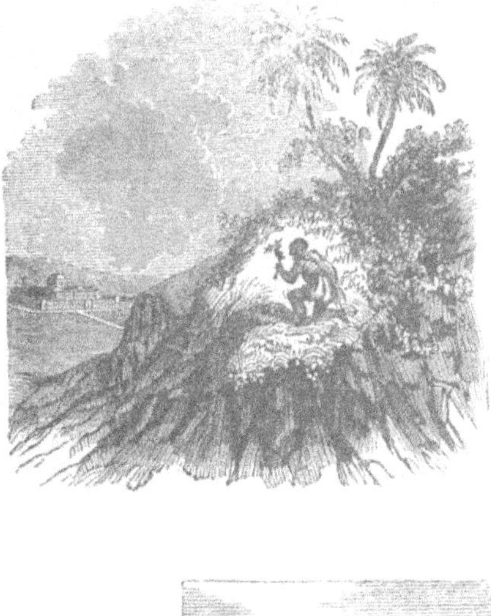

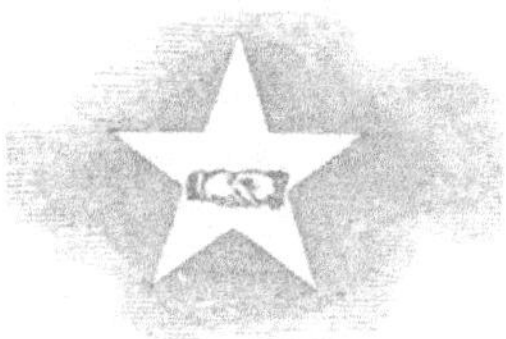

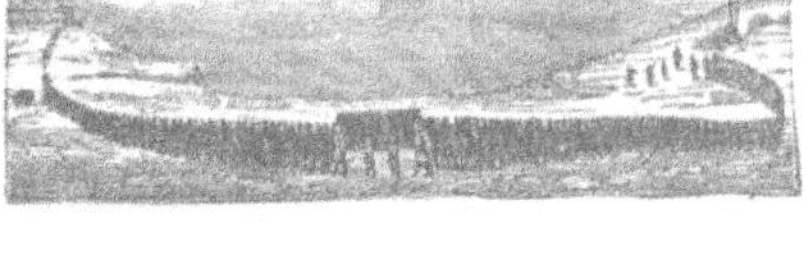

MASTER MASON.—SECOND SECTION.

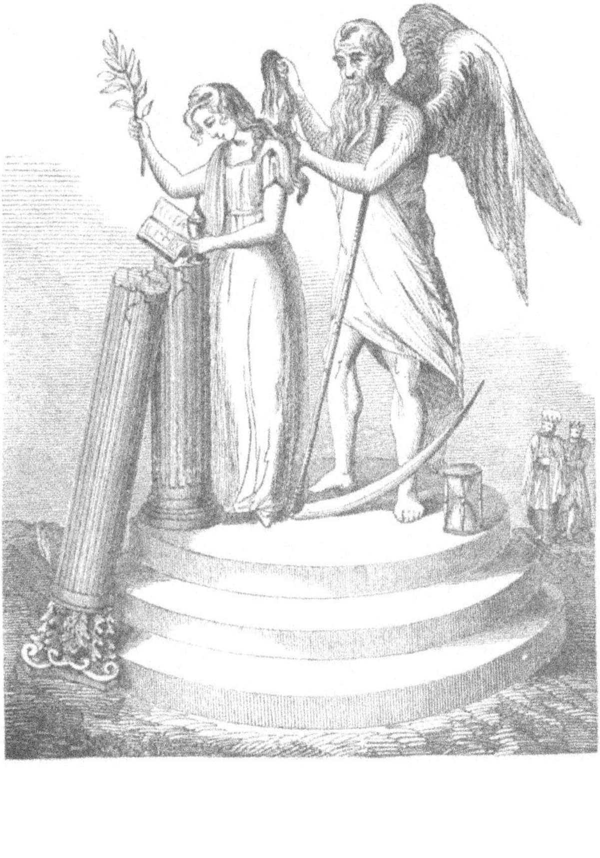

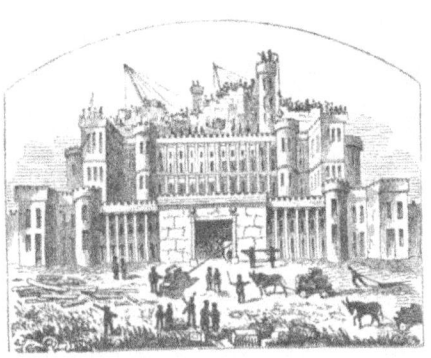

1,453 *Columns.*
2,906 *Pilasters.*
   3 *Grand Masters.*

3,300 *Overseers.*
80,000 *Fellow Crafts.*
70,000 *Entered Apprentices.*

$7 \left\{ \frac{1}{6} \right.$ $5 \left\{ \frac{2}{8} \right.$ 3

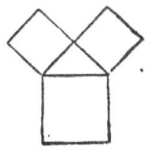

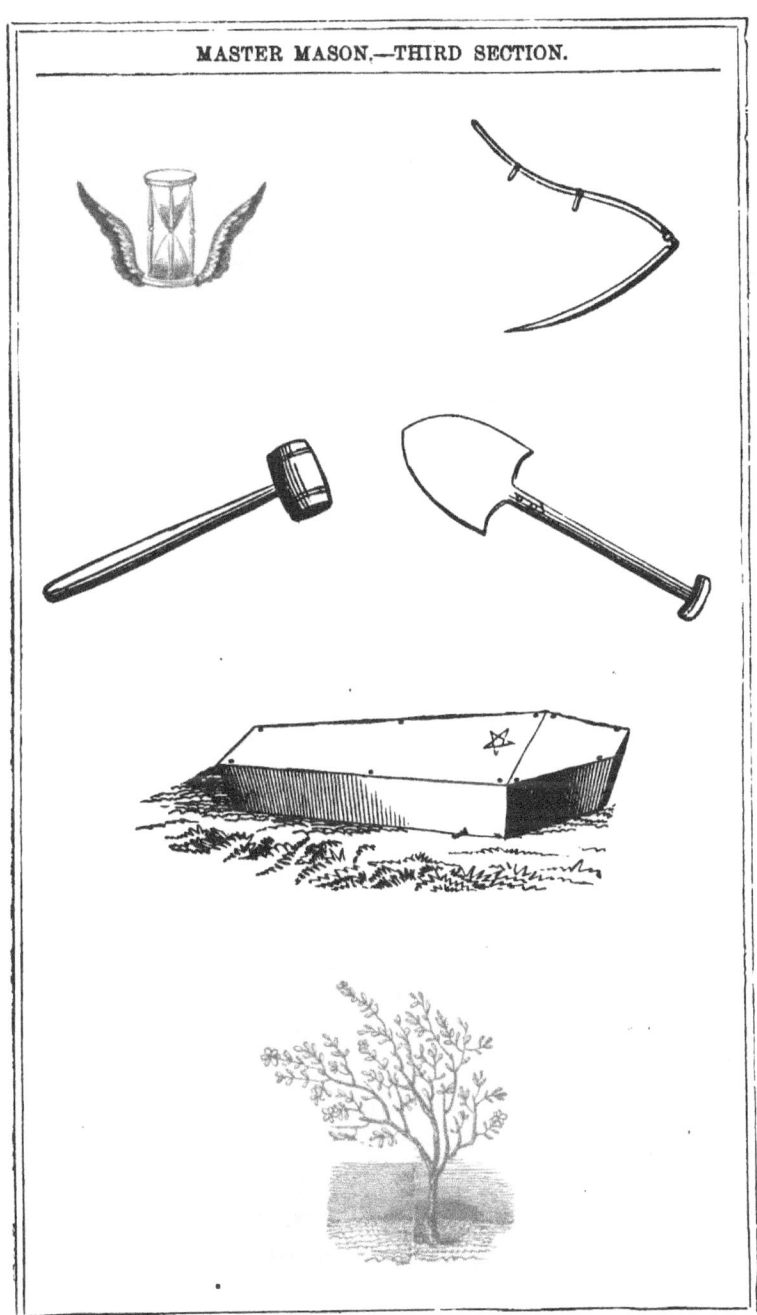

MANUAL OF THE LODGE.

OPENING AND CLOSING THE LODGE.

THE necessity of some preparatory ceremonies, of a more or less formal character, before proceeding to the dispatch of the ordinary business of any association, has always been recognized. Decorum and the dignity of the meeting alike suggest, even in popular assemblies called only for a temporary purpose, that a presiding offi. cer shall with some formality be inducted into the chair, and he then, to use the ordinary phrase, "opens" the meeting with the appointment of his necessary assistance, and with the announcement, in an address to the audience, explanatory of the objects that have called them together.

If secular associations have found it expedient by the adoption of some preparatory forms to avoid the appearance of an unseeming abruptness in proceeding to business, it may well be supposed that religious societies have been still more observant of the custom, and that as their pursuits are more elevated, that the ceremonies of their preparation for the object of their meeting should be still more impressive.

In the Ancient Mysteries (those sacred rites which have furnished so many models for Masonic symbolism), the opening ceremonies were of the most solemn character. The sacred herald, in the Ancient Mysteries, commenced the ceremonies of opening the greater initiations by the solemn formula of " Depart hence, ye profane!" to which was added a proclamation which forbade the use of any language which might be deemed of un favorable augury to the approaching rites.

In like manner a Lodge of Masons is opened with the employment of certain ceremonies in which, that attention may be given to their symbolic as well as practical import, every member present is expected to take a part.

These ceremonies, which slightly differ in each of the degrees—but differ so slightly as not to affect their general character—may be considered in reference to the several purposes which they are designed to affect, to be divided into eight successive steps or parts.

1. The Master having signified his intention to proceed to the labors of the Lodge, every brother is expected to assume his necessary Masonic clothing, and, if an officer, the insignia of his office, and silently and decorously to repair to his appropriate station.

2. The next step in the ceremony is, with the usual precautions, to ascertain the right of each one to be present. It is scarcely necessary to say that in the performance of this duty, the officers who are charged with it should allow no one to remain who is not either well known to themselves or properly vouched for by some discreet and experienced brother.

3. Attention is next directed to the external avenues of the Lodge, and the officers within and without, who are intrusted with the performance of this important duty, are expected to execute it with care and fidelity.

4 By a wise provision, it is no sooner intimated to the Master

that he may safely proceed, than he directs his attention to an inquiry into the knowledge possessed by his officers of the duties that they will be respectively called upon to perform.

5. Satisfied upon this point, the Master then announces, by formal proclamation, his intention to proceed to business; and mindful of the peaceful character of our Institution, he strictly forbids all immoral or unmasonic conduct whereby the harmony of the Lodge may be impeded, under no less a penalty than the by-laws may impose or a majority of the brethren present may see fit to inflict. Nor after this is any brother permitted to leave the Lodge during Lodge hours (that is, from the time of opening to that of closing), without having first obtained the Worshipful Master's permission.

6. Certain mystic rites, which can here be only alluded to, are then employed, by which each brother present signifies his concurrence in the ceremonies which have been celebrated, and his knowledge of the degree in which the Lodge is about to be opened.

7. It is a lesson which every Mason is taught at one of the earliest points of his initiation, that he should commence no important undertaking without first invoking the blessing of Deity. Hence the next step in the progress of the opening ceremonies is to address a prayer to the Supreme Architect of the Universe. This prayer, although offered by the Master, is to be participated in by every brother, and at its conclusion the audible response of "So mote it be: Amen," should be made by all present.

8. The Lodge is then declared, in the name of God and the Holy Saints John, to be opened in due form, on the first, second, or third degree of Masonry, as the case may be.

A Lodge is said to be opened *in the name of God and the Holy Saints John*, as a declaration of the sacred and religious purposes of our meeting, of our profound reverence for that Divine Being whose name and attributes should be the constant themes of our contemplation, and of our respect for those ancient patrons whom the traditions of Masonry have so intimately connected with the history of the Institution.

It is said to be opened *in due form*, to intimate that all that is necessary, appropriate, and usual in the ceremonies, all that the law requires or ancient usage renders indispensable, have been observed.

And it is said to be opened *on*, and not *in*, a certain degree (which latter expression is often incorrectly used), in reference rather to the speculative than to the legal character of the meeting; to indicate, not that the members are to be circumscribed *in* the limits of a particular degree, but that they are met together to unite in contemplation *on* the symbolic teachings and divine lessons, to inculcate which is the peculiar object of that degree.

The ceremony of closing varies but very slightly from that of opening. Of course the first and second steps which have already been enumerated as proper to be observed when the brethren first assemble together, are to be dispensed with when they are about to part, as being under those circumstances entirely unnecessary, and the proclamations and prayers which refer to opening must be varied when they are to be applied to the closing. But in all other respects the ceremonies are the same.

NOTE.—The usage in many jurisdictions permits a Lodge to be closed " in short form " on one degree, for the purpose of being opened in like manner on another degree. This is, however, only to be done when the object is to initiate, pass, or raise a candidate, or when the initiation in an inferior degree having been accomplished, it is necessary to resume labor on the third degree for the transaction of business. Thus the Lodge being open on the third · degree, and it being proposed " to pass " a candidate who is in waiting, the Lodge of Masters may be closed " in short form," and a Lodge opened in like manner on the second degree. The " short form " consists in the omission of all the usual ceremony, except the proclamation by the Master and Wardens.

But a Lodge can never be opened at the beginning of a communication, nor finally closed at its termination, except " in due form."

FORMS OF PRAYER.

PRAYER AT OPENING.

MOST holy and glorious Lord God, the great Architect of the Universe, the giver of all good gifts and graces: Thou hast promised that, "where two or three are gathered together in thy name, thou wilt be in the midst of them, and bless them." In thy name we assemble, most humbly beseeching thee to bless us in all our undertakings, that we may know and serve thee aright, and that all our actions may tend to thy glory, and to our advancement in knowledge and virtue. And we beseech thee, O Lord God, to bless our present assembling, and to illuminate our minds, that we may walk in the light of thy countenance; and when the trials of our probationary state are over, be admitted into THE TEMPLE "not made with hands, eternal in the heavens."

Response by the Brethren.—So mote it be. Amen.

PRAYER AT CLOSING.

Supreme Architect of the Universe, accept our humble praises for the many mercies and blessings which thy bounty has conferred on us, and especially for this friendly and social intercourse. Pardon, we beseech thee, whatever thou hast seen amiss in us since we have been together; and continue to us thy presence, protection, and blessing. Make us sensible of the renewed obligations we are under to love thee supremely, and to be friendly to each other. May all our irregular passions be subdued, and may we daily increase in *Faith*, *Hope*, and *Charity;* but more especially in that *Charity* which is the bond of peace and the perfection of every virtue. May we so practice thy precepts, that we may finally obtain thy promises, and find an entrance through the gates into the temple and city of our God.

Response.—So mote it be. Amen.

BENEDICTION AT CLOSING.

May the blessing of Heaven rest upon us and all regular Masons! May brotherly love prevail, and every moral and social virtue cement us.

Response.—So mote it be. Amen.

In addition to the prayer, it is sometimes customary to use the following:

CHARGE AT CLOSING.

BRETHREN:

We are now about to quit this sacred retreat of friendship and virtue, to mix again with the world. Amidst its concerns and employments, forget not the duties which you have heard so frequently inculcated, and so forcibly recommended in this Lodge. Be diligent, prudent, temperate, discreet. Remember that, around this altar, you have promised to befriend and relieve every brother who shall need your assistance. You have promised, in the most friendly manner, to remind him of his errors, and aid a reformation. These generous principles are to extend further. Every human being has a claim upon your kind offices. Do good unto all. Recommend it more

especially " to the household of the faithful." Finally, brethren, be ye all of one mind ; live in peace ;
and may the God of love and peace deligh to dwell
with and bless you.

PRAYER AT OPENING THE GRAND LODGE.

O ! most glorious and eternal Lord God, the world's
Supreme Architect, the source of light, of life, and
of love, we, thy servants, assembled in solemn Grand
Lodge, would now implore thy gracious protection
and favor.

In thy name, O Lord, we have assembled, and in
thy name we desire to proceed in all our doings. Let
the Spirit of Peace and of Love rest upon us. Let
the wisdom of our sublime Institution so subdue every
discordant passion within us, so harmonize and enrich
our hearts with a portion of thine own love and goodness, that the Grand Lodge, at this time, and at every
time, may be a sincere though humble copy of that
Order, Beauty, and Unity which reign forever before
thy throne.

Enlighten, we beseech thee, the dark corners of the
earth with the rays of our benevolent Institution, that
all the ends of the world may know thee, and every
human being be taught to love his fellow-man.

Let thy protection be over all the members of the
mystic family, wheresoever dispersed, and bless their
lawful labors. Graciously accept these our supplica-
tions and prayers, for the sake of thy most holy and
glorious name.

Response.—So mote it be. Amen.

ENTERED APPRENTICE'S DEGREE.

SYMBOLISM OF THE DEGREE.

HE first degree, or that of the Entered Apprentice, is intended in its symbolic signification to furnish a representation of youth just entering on the struggles, the trials, and duties of an earthly and responsible existence. On his first admission into the Lodge, the candidate is reminded of the weak and helpless state of man on his entrance into the world — unprepared for the exigencies of the present, ignorant of the vicissitudes of the future, and dependent for his safety and very existence on that God in whom alone, in all trials and difficulties, is there any sure and abiding trust.

And as the youth is prepared by a useful and virtuous education for his journey through life, so the Apprentice obtains in his degree those first instructions whereon to erect his future moral and Masonic edifice. He now receives the elementary details of that universal language in which hereafter he is to converse with his brethren of all nations, so as to understand and be understood by Masons of every tongue and dialect under the sun. He is directed to take, as a staff and scrip for his journey, a knowledge of all the virtues that expand the heart and dignify the soul. Secrecy, obedience, humility, trust in God, purity of conscience, economy of time, are all inculcated by symbolic ceremonies too impressive in their character ever to be forgotten. And, lastly, as charity forms the chief corner-stone of all the Masonic virtues, the beauty and holiness of this attribute are depicted in emblematic modes which no spoken language could equal. The degree of the Apprentice is, in short, one of probation and preparation for a more advanced position, and more exalted privileges and duties.

FIRST LECTURE.

The first lecture of Freemasonry, or that appropriated to the degree of an Entered Apprentice, is divided into three sections. In this lecture virtue is painted in the most beautiful colors, and the duties of morality are strictly enforced. In it we are taught such useful lessons as prepare the mind for a regular advancement in the principles of knowledge and philosophy; and these are imprinted on the memory by lively and sensible images, to influence our conduct in the proper discharge of the duties of social life.

Every candidate, before his reception, is required to make the following declarations to the Senior Deacon, in the presence of the Stewards, in a room adjacent to the Lodge.

Do you seriously declare, upon your honor, that, unbiased by the improper solicitation of friends, and uninfluenced by mercenary motives, you freely and voluntarily offer yourself a candidate for the mysteries of Masonry?

I do.

Do you sincerely declare, upon your honor, that you are prompted to solicit the privileges of Masonry by a favorable opinion conceived of the Institution, and a desire of knowledge?

I do.

Do you seriously declare, upon your honor, that you will cheerfully conform to all the ancient usages and established customs of the fraternity?

I do.

FIRST SECTION.

The first section of the Entered Apprentice's Lecture princi pally consists of a recapitulation of the ceremonies of initiation. But, on this account, a knowledge of it is highly necessary to every Mason, that he may be the better enabled to assist in the correct performance of the ritual of the degree. It is, however introduced by some general heads, which qualify us to examine the rights of others to our privileges, while they prove our claims to the character we profess.

It is, of course, impossible, in a monitorial work, to give a full explanation of the various symbols and ceremonies which are used in the inculcation of moral and religious truths; but an allusion, in even general terms, to the most important ones, in the order in which they occur, will be sufficient to lead the con templative Mason to a further examination of their import.

THE SHOCK OF ENTRANCE.

In the symbolic science of Masonry, the Lodge is often repre- sented as a symbol of life. In this case, Lodge labor becomes the symbol of the labor of life, its duties, trials, and temptations, and the Mason is the type of the laborer and actor in that life. The Lodge is, then, at the time of the reception of an Entered Apprentice, a symbol of the world, and the initiation is a type of the new life upon which the candidate is about to enter. There he stands without our portals, on the threshold of this new Masonic life, in darkness, helplessness, and ignorance. Hav- ing been wandering amid the errors and covered over with the pollutions of the outer and profane world, he comes inquiringly to our doors, seeking the new birth, and asking a withdrawal of the vail which conceals divine truth from his uninitiated sight. And here, as with Moses at the burning bush, the solemn admo- nition is given, "Put off thy shoes from off thy feet, for the place whereon thou standest is holy ground;" and ceremonial preparations surround him, all of a significant character, to indi- cate to him that some great change is about to take place in his

mo... and intellectual condition. He is already beginning t >
discover that the design of Masonry is to introduce him to ne w
views of life and its duties. He is, indeed, to commence with
new lessons in a new school. There is to be, not simply a change
for the future, but also an extinction of the past; for initiation
is, as it were, a death to the world and a resurrection to a new
life. And hence it was that among the old Greeks the same
word signified both *to die* and *to be initiated.* But death, to
him who believes in immortality, is but a new birth. Now, this
new birth should be accompanied with some ceremony to indicate symbolically, and to impress upon the mind, this disruption
of old ties and formation of new ones. Hence the impression of
this idea is made by the symbolism of the *shock at the entrance.*
The world is left behind—the chains of error and ignorance
which had previously restrained the candidate in moral and intellectual captivity are to be broken—the portal of the Temple
has been thrown widely open, and Masonry stands before the
neophyte in all the glory of its form and beauty, to be fully revealed to him, however, only when the new birth has been com-
pletely accomplished. Shall this momentous occasion be passed
unnoticed? Shall this great event—the first in the Masonic life
of the aspirant—have no visible or audible record? Shall the
entrance, for the first time, into the Lodge—the birth, as it has
justly been called, into Masonry—be symbolized by no outward
sign? Shall the symbolism of our science, ever ready at all
other times, with its beautiful teachings, here only be dumb and
senseless? Or, rather, shall not all the Sons of Light who witness the impressive scene feel like the children of Korah, who,
when released from the captivity of Babylon, and once more re-
turning to the Temple, exclaimed, in the heart-burst of their
grateful joy, " O, clap your hands all ye people; shout unto God
with the voice of triumph."

The SHOCK OF ENTRANCE is, then, the symbol of the disruption of the candidate from the ties of the world, and his intro
duction into the life of Masonry. *It is the symbol of the agonies
of the first death and of the throes of the new birth.*

PRAYER AT THE INITIATION OF A CANDIDATE.

As Masons, we are taught never to commence any great or important undertaking, without first invoking the blessing of Deity. At the initiation of a candidate it is, therefore, usual to make use of the following

PRAYER.*

Vouchsafe thine aid, Almighty Father of the Universe, to this our present convention, and grant that this candidate for Masonry may dedicate and devote his life to thy service, and become a true and faithful brother among us. Endue him with a competency of thy divine wisdom, that by the secrets of our art he may be better enabled to display the beauties of godliness to the honor of thy holy name. *So mote it be.—* Amen.

THE RITE OF CIRCUMAMBULATION.

The rite of Circumambulation, derived from the Latin verb "circumambulare," *to walk around anything*, is the name given to that observance in all the religious ceremonies of antiquity, which consisted in a procession around an altar or some other sacred object.

Thus, in Greece, the priests and the people, when engaged in their sacrificial rites, always walked three times around the altar while singing a sacred hymn. MACROBIUS tells us that this ceremony had a reference to the motion of the heavenly bodies, which, according to the ancient poets and philosophers, produced

---

* This prayer is found in PRESTON, upon whose authority I have restored the word "godliness" instead of "virtuousness" used by WEBB, or "holiness" adopted by CROSS The prayer, but in a very different form, is, however. much older than PRESTON, who borrowed, abridged, and altered the much longer formula which had been used previous to his day. It is said that the prayer at initiation was a ceremony in use among the "Ancient" or "York Masons." but omitted by the "Moderns"

a harmonious sound, inaudible to mortal ears, which was called "the music of the spheres." Hence, in making this procession around the altar, great care was taken to move in imitation of the apparent course of the sun. For this purpose, they commenced at the east, and proceeding by the way of the south to the west, and thence by the north, they arrived at the east again By this method, it will be perceived that the right side was always nearest to the altar.

Much stress was laid by the ancients on the necessity of keeping the altar on the right hand of the persons moving around, because it was in this way only that the apparent motion of the sun from east to west could be imitated. Thus PLAUTUS, the Roman poet, makes one of his characters say, "If you would do reverence to the gods, you must turn to the right hand;" and GRONOVIUS, in commenting on this passage, says that the ancients, "in worshiping and praying to the gods, were accustomed to turn to the right hand." In one of the hymns of CALLIMACHUS, supposed to have been chanted by the priests of APOLLO, it is said, "We imitate the example of the sun, and follow his benevolent course." VIRGIL describes CORYNÆUS as purifying his companions at the funeral of MISENUS by passing three times around them, and at the same time aspersing them with the lustral water, which action he could not have conveniently performed, unless he had moved with his right hand toward them, thus making his circuit from east to west by the south.

In fact, the ceremony of circumambulation was, among the Romans, so intimately connected with every religious rite of expiation or purification, that the same word, "*lustrare*," came at length to signify both *to purify*, which was its original meaning, and also *to walk around anything*.

Among the Hindoos, the rite of circumambulation was always practiced as a religious ceremony, and a Brahmin, on rising from his bed in the morning, having first adored the sun, while directing his face to the east, then proceeds by the way of the south to the west, exclaiming at the same time, "I follow the course of the sun."

The Druids preserved this rite of circumambulation in their

mystical dance around the *cairn* or altar of sacred stones. On these occasions, the priest always made three circuits, from east to west, around the altar, having it on his right hand, and accompanied by all the worshipers. And this sacred journey was called, in the Celtic language, *Deiseal,* from two words signifying the *right hand* and the *sun,* in allusion to the mystical object of the ceremony and the peculiar manner in which it was performed.

Hence we find, in the universal prevalence of this ceremony and in the invariable mode of passing from the east to the west by the way of the south, with, consequently, the right hand or side to the altar, a pregnant evidence of the common source of all these rites from some primitive origin, to which Freemasonry is also indebted for its existence. The circumambulation among the Pagan nations was referred to the great doctrine of Sabaism, or sun-worship. Freemasonry alone has preserved the primitive meaning, which was a symbolic allusion to the sun as the source of physical light, and the most wonderful work of the Grand Architect of the Universe. The reason assigned for the ceremony in the modern lectures of WEBB and CROSS is absolutely beneath criticism. The Lodge represents the world; the three principal officers represent the sun in his three principal positions—at rising, at meridian, and at setting. The circumambulation, therefore, alludes to the apparent course of the solar orb, through these points, around the world. This is with us its astronomical symbolism. But its intellectual symbolism is, that the circumambulation and the obstructions at various points refer to the labors and difficulties of the student in his progress from intellectual darkness or ignorance to intellectual light or TRUTH.

The following passage of Scripture is used during the ceremony :

Behold, how good and how pleasant it is for brethren to dwell together in unity!

It is like the precious ointment upon the head, that ran down upon the beard, even Aaron's beard ; that went down to the skirts of his garments :

As the dew of Hermon, and as the dew that
descended upon the mountains of Zion : for there the
Lord commanded the blessing, even life for ever.
more.—*Psalm* cxxxiii.

The great teaching of this Psalm is Brotherly Love, that vir
tue which forms the most prominent tenet of the Masonic Order.
And it teaches the lesson, too, precisely as we do, by a symbol,
comparing it to the precious ointment used in the consecration
of the High Priest, whose delightful perfume filled the whole
place with its odor. The ointment was poured upon the head in
such quantity, that, being directed by the anointer in different
ways in the form of a cross, it flowed at length down the beard,
and finally dropped from the flowing skirts of the priestly gar.
ment.

The fifteen Psalms, from the 120th to the 134th, inclusive, of
which this, of course, is one, are called by the Hebrews, " songs
of degrees," because they were sung on the fifteen steps ascend
ing from the court of Israel to the court of the women in the
Temple.

The best commentators think that the 133d Psalm is intended
to represent the exultation of the Priests and Levites returned
from the captivity at Babylon, and again united in the service
of God in the sanctuary. How appropriate, then, is its adoption
in this degree to commemorate the approaching release of a
neophyte from the darkness in which he had been long wander
ing, and his admission into a society whose dwelling-place is
intended as a representation of that glorious Temple at whose
portals the very hymn of rejoicing was formerly sung. The
candidate will not, of course, at the time, understand the allu
sion, but there is a striking analogy between the liberated Jew
going up from the thralldom of Babylon to join once more with
his brethren in the true worship on "the threshing-floor of
Ornan the Jebusite," and the candidate for Masonry, coming out
of the blindness and darkness of the profane world, to search
for light and truth within the sacred precincts of the Lodge.

THE THREE GATES OF THE TEMPLE.

Dr. Dalcho, in his "Orations," has found great fault with he York rite of Masonry, because it has in its ceremonies per petrated the error of furnishing the Temple of Solomon with three gates—one at the south, one at the west, and one at the east—while in truth there was but one gate to the Temple, and that was in the porch at the east end. But the real error lies with Dr. Dalcho, who has mistaken a symbolic allusion for a historical statement. It is not pretended, that because Masonry has adopted the Temple of Jerusalem as the groundwork or elementary form of all its symbols, a Lodge is therefore ever expected, except in a symbolic sense, to be a representative of the Temple. On the contrary, the very situation of a Lodge is the exact reverse of that of the Temple. The entrance of the former is at the west, that of the latter was at the east. The most holy place in a Lodge is its eastern end, that of the Temple was its western extremity.

The fact is, that in Masonry, all allusions to the Temple of Solomon are simply symbolic, and while the great symbol of a material temple, prefiguring a spiritual one, is preserved, no care has ever been taken to obtain correctness of architectural details, or even of strictly historical facts.

The circumambulation and the three supposed gates, referred to and explained in this section of the lecture, are symbolical of the progress of every man in his journey in search of TRUTH, the great object of all Masonic labor, and of the embarrassments and obstructions that he must meet with in that search. Hence our French brethren call this circumambulation *a voyage*, and each voyage is typical of some danger or trial of human life.

THE OBLIGATION OF SECRECY.

The duty of an Entered Apprentice is embraced by the virtues of *silence* and *secrecy*. Speaking of the origin of those duties among Masons in the primitive period of their origin, Brother NICHOLSON* says: "As idolatry prevailed upon the earth

* Lecture on the "Symbolism of Freemasonry." p. 16.

|ummedi-tely after the Deluge], it became necessary for those who held to the worship of the true God to form themselves into a distinct order—not only those who were of the children of Israel, but also others, who retained the traditions of Israel's God, though of Gentile blood. The time arrived when openly to worship the true God was attended with *danger;* and then t was that our brethren had *special* recourse to hieroglyphics nd symbols to preserve secrecy, lest they should be exposed to tre arm of persecution. But as, indeed, the arcana or recondite points of religion were always in possession of the priests alone, among the different idolatrous peoples; and as peculiar forms of initiation were practiced by them, attended with the greatest secrecy (not to say with positive danger to the candidates), the same practice was resorted to by the votaries of the true God, at least so far as secrecy was concerned — secrecy from that time forth ranking as a virtue among Masons, and justly so. Again, to preserve the privileges of the Order, strict secrecy was observed, lest those privileges should become abused. Among the ancients, secrecy stood high as a mark of wisdom.

CALCOTT, also, on this subject says: "If we turn our eyes back to antiquity, we shall find that the old Egyptians had so great a regard for *silence* and *secrecy* in the mysteries of their religion, that they set up the god HARPOCRATES, to whom they paid particular honor and veneration, who was represented with his right hand placed near the heart, and the left down by his side, covered with a skin, before full of eyes and ears, to signify that, of many things to be seen and heard, few are to be *published*"

THE UNWRITTEN LANDMARKS.

The instructions which constitute the hidden or esoteric knowledge in Freemasonry are forbidden to be written, and can only be communicated by oral intercourse of one Mason with another. This is another instance of the great antiquity of the usages of Freemasonry, which is presenting such collateral evidences of its venerable age.

In all the ancient mysteries, the same reluctance to commit the esoteric instructions of the hierophants to writing is apparent and hence the secret knowledge taught in their initiations was preserved in symbols, the true meaning of which was closely concealed from the profane.

The Druids had a similar regulation; and Cæsar informs us that it was not considered lawful to intrust their sacred verses to writing; but these were always committed to memory by their disciples.

The same custom prevailed among the Jews with respect to the Oral Law, which was never intrusted to books; but, being preserved in the memories of the priests and wise men, was handed down, from one to the other, through a long succession of ages.

MAIMONIDES has described, according to the Rabbinical traditions, the mode adopted by MOSES to impress the principles of this Oral Law.

The secret doctrine of the Cabala, or the mystical philosophy of the Hebrews, was, also, communicated in an oral form, and, says MAURICE, "transmitted, verbally, down to all the great characters celebrated in Jewish antiquity—among whom both DAVID and SOLOMON were deeply conversant in its most hidden mysteries. Nobody, however, had ventured to commit anything of this kind to paper."

The Christian Church, in the age immediately succeeding the Apostolic, observed the same custom of oral instruction. The early Fathers were eminently cautious not to commit certain of the mysterious dogmas of their religion to writing, lest the surrounding pagans should be made acquainted with what they could neither understand nor appreciate. ST. BASIL, treating of this subject, in the fourth century, says: "We receive the dogmas transmitted to us by writing and those which have descended to us from the Apostles, beneath the mystery of oral tradition; for several things have been handed to us without writing, lest the vulgar, too familiar with our dogmas, should lose a due respect for them."

A custom so ancient as this, of keeping the landmarks unwritten, and one so invariably observed by the Masonic fraternity, we may very naturally presume, must have been originally established with the wisest intentions; and as the usage was adopted by many other institutions, whose organization was similar to that of Freemasonry, we may also suppose that it was connected with the character of an esoteric instruction.

The following passage of Scripture is here used:

In the beginning God created the heavens and the earth. And the earth was without form, and void; and darkness was upon the face of the deep. And the Spirit of God moved upon the face of the waters. And God said, Let there be Light: and there was Light.

THE SHOCK OF ENLIGHTENMENT.

The material light which sprung forth at the fiat of the **Grand Architect**, when darkness and chaos were dispersed, has ever been, in Masonry, a favorite symbol of that intellectual illumination which it is the object of the Order to create in the minds of its disciples, whence we have justly assumed the title of "Sons of Light." This mental illumination—this spiritual light, which, after his new birth, is the first demand of the candidate, is but another name for Divine Truth—the truth of God and the soul—the nature and essence of both—which constitute the chief design of all Masonic teaching. And as the chaos and confusion in which, "in the beginning," the earth, "without form, and void," was enwrapt were dispersed, and order and beauty established by the Supreme command which created material light; so, at the proper declaration, and in the due and recognized form, the intellectual chaos and confusion in which the mind of the neophyte is involved are dispersed, and the true knowledge of the science and philosophy, the faith and doctrine of Masonry, are developed.

But what mind can conceive, or what pen portray, that terrible convulsion of nature, that awful disentanglement of its elements, which must have accompanied the Divine command, "Let there be light!" The attempt to describe it would be a presumptuous task. We feel, when we meditate on the subject, that stillness and silence must have fled before the Almighty Voice, and the earth itself have trembled in its new existence, when the gloomy pall of darkness was rolled as a curtain from the face of nature.

And in Masonry, by the *Shock of Enlightenment*, we seek, humbly, indeed, and at an inconceivable distance, to preserve the recollection and to embody the idea of the birth of material light by the representation of the circumstances that accompanied it, and their reference to the birth of intellectual or Masonic light. The one is the type of the other; and hence the illumination of the candidate is attended with a ceremony that may be supposed to imitate the primal illumination of the universe—most feebly, it is true, and yet not altogether without impressiveness.

The *Shock of Enlightenment* is, then, a symbol of the change which is now taking place in the intellectual condition of the candidate. *It is the symbol of the birth of intellectual light and the dispersion of intellectual darkness.*

The Holy Bible is given to us as the rule and guide of our faith; the Square, to square our actions; and the Compasses, to circumscribe our desires and passions in due bounds with all mankind, but more especially with brother Masons; and hence the Bible is the light which enlightens the path of our duty to God; the Square, that which enlightens the path of duty to our fellow-men; and the Compasses, that which enlightens the path of our duty to ourselves.

The lesser lights are intended to remind us of that symbolism which makes the Lodge a type of the world; and hence the

Master, presiding and dispensing light, may well be compared to those heavenly luminaries which were made, "the greater light to rule the day, and the lesser light to rule the night;" and we are thus reminded, that as the sun rules the day and the moon governs the night, so should the W. M. rule and govern his Lodge with equal regularity and precision.

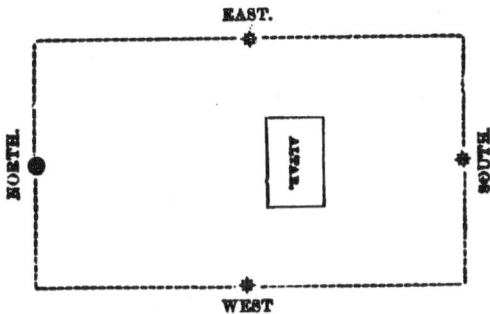

NOTE.—Errors are so often made in placing the lights around the altar, that the preceding diagram is inserted for the direction of the Senior Deacon, whose duty it is to see that they are properly distributed. The stars represent the positions of the lights in the E., W., and S., and the black dot, the place of darkness in the N., where there is no light. The dotted line passing through these points in the diagram represents the limits of the Lodge, and shows that the lights are in the proper cardinal points.

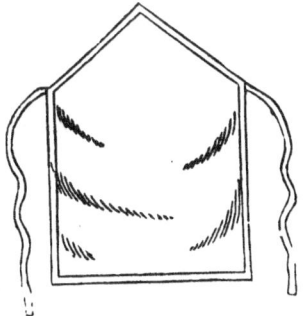

When being clothed as an Entered Apprentice, the candidate receives the following charge:

I present you with this *lambskin* or *white leather apron*, which is an emblem of innocence and the badge of a Mason, more ancient than the Gold in Fleece* or Roman Eagle ;† more honorable than the Star and Garter,‡ or any other order that could be conferred upon you, at this or any other future period, by king, prince, or potentate, or any other person. except he were a Mason and in the body of a Lodge, and which, I trust, you will wear with equal pleasure to yourself and honor to the fraternity.

THE LAMBSKIN APRON.

The use of the apron, or some equivalent mode of investiture as a mystic symbol, was common to all the religious systems of antiquity. Among the Israelites, the girdle formed a part of the investiture of the priesthood. In the Persian mysteries of MITHRAS the candidate was invested with a white apron. In the Brahminical initiations of Hindostan, the Zennaar, or sacred Lord, was substituted for the apron. The Essenians clothed their novices with a white robe. Even the Japanese, in their rites of initiation, invest their candidate with a white apron.

The *color* of a Mason's apron should be *pure white*, because this color has in all ages and countries been deemed an emblem of purity and innocence. Thus, in the early ages of the Christian Church, the newly-baptized convert was invested with a white robe, to denote that he had been cleansed from his former sins, and was thenceforth to lead a life of purity. With a similar meaning, the same undefiled color has been preserved in the apron of the Freemason.

The *material* of a Mason's apron must be *lambskin*. No other

---

* The Order of the Golden Fleece was an order of knighthood instituted in 1429, by Philip, Duke of Burgundy.

† There is no such order as the Knights of the Roman Eagle. The expression (which is an unhappy one) probably refers to the fact that the Eagle was the standard of the ancient Roman Empire.

‡ The Order of the Garter, the most noble of the British orders of knighthood, was instituted in 1344, by Edward III. The Star and the Garter are the insignia bestowed upon and worn by a knight.

substance, such as linen, silk, or satin, can be sub stituted, with out entirely destroying the symbolic character of the apron, be cause the lamb has in all ages been deemed the appropriate em- blem of innocence.

The true Masonic apron should, then, be of unspotted lamb- skin, from 14 to 16 inches wide, and from 12 to 14 inches deep, with a fall ab ut 3 or 4 inches deep, square at the bottom, with sharp angular corners, and without device or ornament of any kind. The usage of the craft in this country has, within a few years past, allowed a narrow edging of blue ribbon, in allusion to that universal friendship which is the bond of the Society, and of which virtue blue is the symbol. But this, undoubtedly, is an innovation, for the ancient apron was without any edging or ornament. All extraneous ornaments and devices are in bad taste, and d tract from the symbolic character of the investiture. But the silk or satin aprons, bespangled, and painted, and em- broidered, which have been gradually creeping into our Lodges, have no sort of connection with Ancient Craft Masonry. They are an innovation of French origin, which should be persistently discouraged by all who admire the simplicity and beauty of our symbols. A Mason who duly and truly appreciates the symbolic meaning of his apron would no more tolerate a linen one for its economy, or an embroidered satin one for its decorations, than an artist would a gilded statue. The lambskin, and the lamb- skin alone, is the badge "more ancient than the Golden Fleece or Roman Eagle, and more honorable than the Star and Garter."

THE NORTHEAST CORNER.

In the important ceremony which refers to the northeast corner of the Lodge, the candidate becomes as one who is to all out ward appearance *a perfect and upright man and Mason*, the representative of a spiritual corner-stone, on which he is to erect his future moral and Masonic edifice.

This symbolic reference of the corner-stone of a material edi fice to a Mason when, at his first initiation, he commences the moral and intellectual task of erecting a spiritual temple in his heart, is beautifully sustained when we look at all the qualities that are required to constitute a " well-tried, true, and trusty" corner-stone. The squareness of its surface, emblematic of morality—its cubical form, emblematic of firmness and stability of character—and the peculiar finish and fineness of the material, emblematic of virtue and holiness—show that the ceremony of the northeast corner of the Lodge was undoubtedly intended to portray, in the consecrated language of symbolism, the necessity of integrity and stability of conduct, of truthfulness and uprightness of character, and of purity and holiness of life, which just at that time and in that place the candidate is most impressively charged to maintain.

THE WORKING TOOLS.

The working tools of an Entered Apprentice are the *Twenty-four-inch Guage* and the *Common Gavel.*

The *Twenty-four-inch Guage* is an instrument used by operative masons to measure and lay cut their w rk ; but we, as Free and Accepted Masons, are taught to make use of it for the more noble and glorious purpose of dividing our time. It being divided into twenty-four equal parts, is emblematical of the twenty-four hours of the day, which we are taught to divide into three equal parts; whereby are found eight hours for the service of God and a distressed worthy brother ; eight for our usual vocations and eight for refreshment and sleep.

The *Common Gavel* is an instrument made use of by operative masons to break off the corners of rough stones, the better to fit them for the builder's use ; but we, as Free and Accepted Masons, are taught to make use of it for the more noble and glorious purpose of divesting our hearts and consciences of all the vices and superfluities of life ; thereby fitting our minds as living stones for that spiritual building, that house "not made with hands, eternal in the heavens."

This presentation of the working tools of a stone-mason to the candidate must necessarily attract his attention to the fact that there is a connection between the operative art and the speculative science, which connection simply consists in this, that speculative Masonry is the application and sanctification of the working tools and implements, the rules and principles of operative masonry, to the veneration of God and the purification of the heart.

The Operative Masons at Jerusalem, from whom we date our origin, were occupied in the construction of an earthly and material temple, to be dedicated to the service and worship of God—a house in which the mighty Jehovah was to dwell visibly by his Shekinah, and whence he was, by Urim and Thummin, to send forth his oracles for the government and direction of his chosen people.

The Speculative Mason is engaged in the construction of a spiritual temple in his heart, pure and spotless, fit for the dwelling-place of Him who is the author of purity ; where God is to be worshiped in spirit and in truth, and whence every evil thought and unruly passion are to be banished, as the sinner and the Gentile were excluded from the sanctuary of the Jewish Temple.

In the symbolic language of Masonry, therefore, the twenty-four-inch guage is a symbol of time well employed; the common gavel, of the purification of the heart.

In the Ancient Mysteries, the first step taken by the candidate was a lustration or purification. The candidate was not permitted to enter the sacred vestibule, or to take any part in the secret formula of initiation, until by water or fire he was emblematically purified from the corruptions of the world which he was about to leave behind. A similar principle exists in Freemasonry where the first symbols presented to the Entered Apprentice are those which inculcate a purification of the heart, of which the purification of the body in the Ancient Mysteries was symbolic

We no longer make use of the bath or the fountain, because in our philosophical system the symbolism is more abstract; but we present the candidate with the *apron*, the *guage*, and the *gavel*, as symbols, of a spiritual purification. The design is the same, but the mode in which it is accomplished is different.

In former times, before the general use of writing, men were accustomed to avail themselves of any imperishable substance as a memorial of some transaction, the record of which would now be committed to paper or parchment. Hence we find in the primitive Christian Church, that a fish-shaped die was used as a certificate of membership, and was so recognized from town to town and from church to church. Especially was a piece of metal or ivory made use of by the ancients as a token of a pledge of amity. Being broken into two pieces, the host, when he had entertained a stranger who was about to depart, gave the guest one part while he retained the other; and these broken pieces served in all times afterward as a memorial of the pledge of friendship that had been thus inaugurated. It may be that the Masonic custom of asking for the deposit of something of the kind in the ARCHIVES OF THE LODGE as a memorial, may have reference to this custom. The candidate is supposed to be thus giving his pledge of fidelity to the Institution. But the subsequent part of the ceremony would teach him that no material and tangible pledge is really wanted, but that the true pledge of Masonic friendship is deposited in the heart. At a future period, in the next section, an opportunity is taken to exemplify the practical application of the pledge thus made, by an impressive charge on the nature of charity.

SECOND SECTION.

The second section of the first lecture, according to the system prevailing in this country, is occupied with an explanation of the symbolic meaning of the ceremonies that are detailed in the first; without, therefore, a knowledge of the second section, the first becomes barren and insignificant. It must, however, be confessed that many of the interpretations given in this section are unsatisfactory to the cultivated mind, and seem to have been adopted on the principle of the old Egyptians, who made use of symbols to conceal rather than to express their thoughts. Learned Masons have been, therefore, always disposed to go beyond the mere technicalities and stereotyped phrases of the lectures, and to look in the history and the philosophy of the ancient religions, and the organization of the ancient mysteries, for a true explanation of most of the symbols of Masonry, and there they have always been enabled to find this true interpretation. The usual lecture is, however, still preserved as a brief mode of acquiring a general knowledge of the mode of Masonic instruction, and as furnishing sufficient proof of the definition that "Freemasonry is a system of morality vailed in allegory and illustrated by symbols."[*]

* WEBB, CROSS, HARDIE, and our other monitorial writers, have printed very little of this section, although they have been exceedingly liberal in their publication of the third section. I have not deemed it expedient to go much beyond their degree of reticence, but I have taken occasion, as being much more useful, to invite attention to the coincidences existing between the ceremonies of Masonry and those of the ancient systems of initiation. The allusions, where I have felt constrained to be cautious in my language, will be well understood by the Mason who has made himself acquainted with the authorized lecture of the degree

PREPARATION.

There is much analogy between the preparation of the candidate in Masonry and the preparation for entering the Temple, as practiced among the ancient Israelites. The Talmudical treatise entitled "Beracoth" prescribes the regulation in these words: "No man shall enter into the Lord's house with his staff [an offensive weapon], nor with his outer garment, nor with shoes on his feet, nor with money in his purse."

*   *   *   *   *   *   *

Various passages of Scripture are referred to in this section as elucidating the traditions of Masonry on the subject of the Temple.

And we will cut wood out of Lebanon, as much as thou shalt need; and we will bring it to thee in floats by sea to Joppa; and thou shalt carry it up to Jerusalem.—2 *Chron.* ii. 16.

And the house, when it was in building, was built of stone made ready before it was brought thither: so that there was neither hammer, nor axe, nor any tool of iron heard in the house, while it was in building.—1 *Kings* vi. 7.

Josephus says: "The whole structure of the Temple was made with great skill, of polished stones, and those laid together so very harmoniously and smoothly, that there appeared to the spectators no sign of any hammer or other instrument of architecture, but as if, without any use of them, the entire materials had naturally united themselves together, so that the agreement of one part with another seemed rather to have been natural, than to have arisen from the force of tools upon them."

*   *   *   *   *   *   *

Now this was the manner in former time in Israel concerning redeeming and concerning changing, for to confirm all things; a man plucked off his shoe, and gave it to his neighbor: and this was a testimony in Israel.—*Ruth* iv. 7.

In the Ancient Mysteries the aspirant was always kept for a certain period in a condition of darkness. Hence darkness became the symbol of initiation. Applied to Masonic symbolism, it is intended to remind the candidate of his ignorance, which Masonry is to enlighten; of his evil nature, which Masonry is to purify; of the world, in whose obscurity he has been wandering, and from which Masonry is to rescue him.

Ask, and it shall be given you; seek, and ye shall find; knock, and it shall be opened unto you.—*Matthew* vii. 7.

In the ancient initiations the candidate was never permitted to enter on the threshold of the temple or sacred cavern in which the ceremonies were to be conducted, until by the most solemn warning he had been impressed with the necessity of caution, secrecy, and fortitude.

PRAYER.

As Masons, we are taught never to commence any great or important undertaking without first invoking the blessing and protection of Deity, and this is because Masonry is a religious institution, and we thereby show our dependence on and our trust in God.

A BELIEF IN GOD.

This constitutes the sole creed of a Mason—at least, the only creed that he is required to profess. But such a profession is essentially and absolutely necessary, because, without a belief in a superintending Power, with the inevitable deduction from the purity and holiness of such a Being, that sin will be punished and virtue rewarded, there would be no sanction to a moral law, for the atheist would have no motive to keep a promise or to preserve an obligation.

THE LEFT SIDE.

The *left side* has always, apparently for a well-known physical reason, been deemed inferior to the right. The right side is the side of honor. "To sit on the right side of the king" was a mark of great favor. And the ancients were so impressed with this fact, that among them the words for *left* and *unlucky* were synonymous, as were also those for *right* and *fortunate*. The same peculiarity exists in our own language, where *sinister* means both *left* and *inauspicious*.

THE RIGHT HAND.

The *right hand* has in all ages been deemed an emblem of fidelity, and our ancient brethren worshiped Deity under the name of Fides or Fidelity, which was sometimes represented by two right hands joined, and sometimes by two human figures, holding each other by the right hands. * * * *

NUMA was the first who erected an altar to FIDES, under which name the goddess of oaths and honesty was worshiped. Obligations taken in her name were considered as more inviolable than any others.*

THE BADGE OF A MASON.

The lamb has in all ages been deemed an emblem of innocence ; by the lambskin, the Mason is therefore reminded of that purity of life and conduct which is so essentially necessary to his gaining admission into the celestial Lodge above, where the Supreme Architect of the Universe presides.

THE FIRST INSTRUCTIONS.

The candidate receives those first instructions whereon to erect his future moral and Masonic edifice in a particular part of the Lodge, because as on the night of his initiation he commences the great task, which is never in his future Masonic life to be discontinued, of erecting in his heart a spiritual temple for the indwelling of God, of which the great material Temple at Jerusalem was but the symbol ; and as each new duty which he learns, and each new virtue that he practices, becomes a living stone in that temple, it is proper that, respecting the whole system of symbolism, he should begin the labor of erecting a spiritual temple just as the operative mason would commence the construction of his material temple, by first laying the corner-stone on which the future edifice is to arise. His first instructions constitute that corner-stone, and on it, when laid in its proper place, he constructs the moral and Masonic temple of his life.

THE LESSON OF CHARITY.

Although Freemasonry is indebted for its origin to its religious and philosophic character, yet charity, in the ordinary

---

* MONTFAUCON mentions several medals in which FIDES was represented by two hands joined together, which, he says, " was the most usual symbol "

adaptation of relief of the distressed, becomes, although inci
dentally, a prominent feature in its teachings. And hence it has
been well said, that there is no institution whose laws more
strongly enforce, or whose precepts more earnestly inculcate, the
virtue of charity. In allusion to the ceremony now under consideration, TANNEHILL remarks that " it is among the first lessons
we are taught, when we pass the threshold of the mystic temple."

THIRD SECTION.

The third section of the Entered Apprentice's lecture explains
the nature and principles of our constitution, and furnishes many
interesting details relating to the Form, Supports, Covering,
Furniture, Ornaments, Lights, and Jewels of a Lodge, how it
should be situated, and to whom dedicated.

Nearly the whole of this section has been made monitorial.
WEBB, and after him CROSS, HARDIE, TANNEHILL, and all other
monitorial writers, have left but little of it unpublished. I have,
on the same principle, slightly increased the amount of information given, by the publication of one or two passages, hitherto
excepted from publication in other monitors, since I could dis
cover no reason why this exception should have been made.

A Lodge is an assemblage of Masons duly congregated, having the Holy Bible, Square, and Compasses,
and a Charter or Warrant of Constitution authorizing
them to work.

Every lawful assemblage of Masons, duly congregated for
work, will be " a just and legally constituted Lodge." It is *just*
that is, *regular* and *orderly*, when it contains the requisite number

to form a quorum, and when the Bible, Square, and Compasses are present. It is *legally constituted* when it is acting under the authority of a Warrant of Constitution, which is an instrument written and printed on parchment or paper (but properly it should be on the former), emanating from the Grand Lodge in whose jurisdiction the Lodge is situated, and signed by the grand officers, which authorizes the persons therein named, and their successors, to meet as Masons and perform Masonic labor. As no assemblage of Masons is legal without such an instrument, it is not only the privilege, but the duty, of every Mason on his first visit to a strange Lodge, to demand a sight of its Warrant of Constitution; nor should any brother sit in a Lodge whose members are unwilling to exhibit the authority on which they act.

Our ancient brethren met on the highest hills and in the lowest valleys, the better to observe the approach of cowans and eavesdroppers, and to guard against surprise.

The reason assigned in the lecture for this assembling on high places, is the modern, but not the true one. The fact is, that mountains and other high places were almost always considered as holy, and peculiarly appropriate for religious purposes, and we have abundant evidence in Scripture that the Jews were accus tomed to worship on the tops of the highest hills, as it was b lieved that sacrifices offered from these elevated places were most acceptable to the Deity. HUTCHINSON says that "the highest hills and the lowest valleys were, from the earliest times, es teemed sacred, and it was supposed that the Spirit of God was peculiarly diffusive in those places."

A Lodge is said, symbolically, to extend in length from east to west; in breadth, from north to south; in height, from the earth to the highest heavens; in depth, from the surface to the center. And a Lodge is said to be of these vast dimensions to denote the universality of Masonry, and to teach us that a Mason's charity should be equally as extensive

There is a peculiar fitness in this theory, which is really only making the Masonic Lodge a symbol of the world. It must be

remembered that, at the era of the Temple, the earth was sup
posed to have the form of a parallelogram, or "oblong square."
Such a figure inscribed upon a map of the world, and including
only that part of it which was known in the days of Solomon,
would present just such a square, embracing the Mediterranean
Sea and the countries lying immediately on its northern, southern, and eastern borders. Beyond, far in the north, would be
the Cimmerian deserts as a place of darkness, while the pillars
of Hercules in the west, on each side of the Straits of Gades—
now Gibraltar—might appropriately be referred to the two pillars that stood at the porch of the Temple. Thus the world itself would be the true Mason's Lodge, in which he was to live
and labor. Again; the solid contents of the earth below, "from
the surface to the center," and the profound expanse above,
"from the earth to the highest heavens," would give to this
parallelogram the outlines of a double cube, and meet thereby
that definition which says, that "the form of the Lodge ought
to be a double cube, as an expressive emblem of the powers of
light and darkness in the creation."*

A Lodge has three principal supports, which are
Wisdom, *Strength*, and *Beauty*, because it is necessary
that there should be wisdom to contrive, strength to
support, and beauty to adorn all great and important
undertakings. Of these, the column of Wisdom is

* OLIVER, Landmarks, l . n. 135, *note* 87

situated in the east part of the Lodge, and is represented by the W∴ M∴ because it is presumed that he
has wisdom to devise labor for the craft, and to superintend them during the hours thereof; the column of
Strength is situated in the west part of the Lodge,
and is represented by the S∴ W∴ because it is his
duty to strengthen and support the authority of the
Master; and the column of Beauty is situated in the
south part of the Lodge, and is represented by the
J∴ W∴ because from his position in the S∴ he is the
first to observe the meridian sun, which is the beauty
and glory of the day, to call the craft from labor to
refreshment, to superintend them during the hours
thereof, to see that none convert the purposes of
refreshment into those of intemperance or excess,
and to call them on again in due season, that the
M∴ W∴ may have honor, and they pleasure and profit
thereby.

The idea that the Lodge is a symbol of the world, is still car
ried out. It was the belief of the ancients that the heavens, or
the roof of the world, was supported by pillars. By these pil
lars, some suppose that the mountains are alluded; but in ref
erence to a passage in Job xxvi. 11, where it is said, "The
pillars of heaven tremble," Noyes thinks that "it is more prob
able that heaven is represented as an immense edifice, supported
on lofty columns, like a temple." But on this passage Dr. Cut
bush is still more explicit. He says: "The arch, in this instance, is allegorical not only of the arch of heaven, but of the
higher degree of Masonry, commonly called the Holy Roya
Arch. The pillars which support the arch are emblematical of
wisdom and strength—the former denoting the wisdom of the
Supreme Architect, and the latter the stability of the universe."—
Brewster's Encyclop., American edition.

Its covering is no less than a clouded canopy or
starry decked heaven, where all good Masons hope at
last to arrive, by the aid of that theological ladder
which Jacob, in his vision, saw ascending from earth

to heaven, the three principal rounds of which are denominated *Faith, Hope,* and *Charity,* and which admonish us to have faith in God, hope of immortality, and charity to all mankind.

The greatest of these is Charity; for our Faith may be lost in sight; Hope ends in fruition; but Charity extends beyond the grave, through the boundless realms of eternity.

The Lodge continues throughout this degree to be presented to the initiate as a symbol of the world, and hence its covering is figuratively supposed to be the "clouded canopy" on which the host of stars is represented. If the Lodge represent the world, then its covering must be represented by the blue vault of heaven.

The mystical ladder which is here referred to, is a symbol that was widely diffused among the religions of antiquity, where, as in Masonry, it was always supposed to consist of seven steps, because seven was a sacred number. In some of the Ancient Mysteries, the seven steps represented the seven planets, and then the *sun* was the topmost; in others they represented the seven metals, and then *gold* was the topmost; in the Brahminical mysteries they represented the seven worlds which constituted the Indian universe, and then the world of *Truth* was the highest. The seven steps of the Masonic ladder are *Temperance, Fortitude, Prudence, Justice, Faith, Hope,* and *Charity;* that is, the four cardinal and the three theological virtues. Now, as charity is love, and as the sun represents Divine Love, and as also the astronomical sign of the sun is gold, and as truth is the synonym of God, it is evident that the topmost round in all these ladders, whether it be the sun, or gold, or truth, or charity, conveys exactly the same lesson of symbolism, namely, that the Mason, living and working in the world as his Lodge, must seek to raise himself out of it to that eminence which surmounts it, where alone he can find DIVINE TRUTH.

The furniture of a Lodge consists of a Holy Bible, Square, and Compasses.

The Holy Bible is dedicated to God; the Square, to the Master; and the Compasses, to the craft.

The Bible is dedicated to God, because it is the inestimable gift of God to man; * * * the Square, to the Master, because it is the proper Masonic emblem of his office; and the Compasses, to the craft, because, by a due attention to their use, they are taught to circumscribe their desires, and keep their passions within due bounds.

The ornaments of a Lodge are the *Mosaic Pavement*, the *Indented Tessel*, and the *Blazing Star*. The Mosaic pavement is a representation of the ground floor of King Solomon's Temple; and the indented tessel, of that beautiful tesselated border or skirting which surrounded it.

The Mosaic pavement is emblematical of human life, checkered with good and evil; the beautiful border which surrounds it is emblematical of those manifold blessings and comforts which surround us, and which we hope to obtain by a faithful reliance on Divine Providence, which is hieroglyphically represented by the blazing star in the center.

Mosaic Pavements, consisting of stones of various colors, so disposed as to represent different shapes or forms, were common in the temples of the ancients. FELLOWS says that they represented the variegated face of the earth in the places where the

ancients formerly held their religious assemblies. The true derivation of the word is unknown, or at least unsettled.

The *Indented Tessel* is a border of stones, of various colors, placed around the pavement. *Tessel*, from the Latin *tessela*, means a little square stone, and *to indent* is to cut or notch a margin into inequalities resembling teeth. A *tesselated border* is, therefore, a notched border of variegated colors.

The *Blazing Star* is said by WEBB to be "commemorative of the star which appeared to guide the wise men of the East to the place of our Savior's nativity." This, which is one of the ancient interpretations of the symbol, being considered as too sectarian in its character, and unsuitable to the universal religion of Masonry, has been omitted since the meeting of Grand Lecturers at Baltimore, in 1842.

A Lodge has three symbolic lights ; one of these is in the East, one in the West, and one in the South. There is no light in the north, because King Solomon's Temple, of which every Lodge is a representation, was placed so far north of the ecliptic, that the sun and moon, at their meridian height, could dart no rays into the northern part thereof. The north we therefore masonically call a place of darkness.

The three lights, like the three principal officers and the three principal supports, refer undoubtedly to the three stations of the sun—its rising in the east, its meridian in the south, and its setting in the west—and thus the symbolism of the Lodge, as typical of the world, continues to be preserved.

The use of lights in all religious ceremonies is an ancient custom. There was a seven-branched candlestick in the tabernacle, and in the Temple " were the golden candlesticks, five on the right and five on the left." They were always typical of moral, spiritual, or intellectual light.

A Lodge has six jewels; three of these are immov able and three movable.

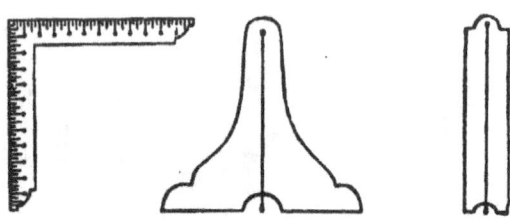

The immovable jewels are the *Square*, *Level*, and *Plumb*.

The square inculcates morality; the level, equality; and the plumb, rectitude of conduct.

They are called immovable jewels, because they are always to be found in the East, West, and South parts of the Lodge, being worn by the officers in those respective stations.

The movable jewels are the *Rough Ashlar*, the *Perfect Ashlar*, and the *Trestle-Board*.*

The rough ashlar is a stone as taken from the quarry in its rude and natural state.

* Such is the division of the jewels in the Lodges of this country; but in English Lodges the reverse is the case; there the rough and perfect ashlars and the trestle-board are the immovable jewels, and the square, level, and plumb are the movable, because they descend from one set of ████ to their successors.

The perfect ashlar is a stone made ready by the hands of the workmen, to be adjusted by the working tools of the fellow-craft. The trestle-board is for the master workman to draw his designs upon.

By the rough ashlar we are reminded of our rude and imperfect state by nature; by the perfect ashlar, that state of perfection at which we hope to arrive by a virtuous education, our own endeavors, and the blessing of God; and by the trestle-board we are also reminded that, as the operative workman erects his temporal building agreeably to the rules and designs laid down by the master on his trestle-board, so should we, both operative and speculative, endeavor to erect our spiritual building agreeably to the rules and designs laid down by the Supreme Architect of the Universe, in the great books of nature and revelation, which are our spiritual, moral, and masonic trestle-board.

To every Mason, whatever may be his peculiar religious creed, that revelation of the Deity which is recognized by his religion becomes his trestle-board. Thus, the trestle-board of the Jewish Mason is the Old Testament; of the Christian, the Old and the New; of the Mohammedan, the Koran. But as no operative mason can work without a trestle-board, where the designs and instructions of his master for his conduct in the building on which he is engaged may be delineated, so no speculative mason can labor truly and profitably in the great work of life without a trestle-board which may contain the delineation of the designs and will of his Eternal Master. And thus it is that, as the atheist acknowledges no such Master, and can therefore have no such trestle board, he is not permitted to unite with us in our "moral, spiritual, and masonic" labor. And this is really the reason of the law which forbids the initiation of atheists.

A Lodge is situated due east and west, because when Moses crossed the Red Sea, being pursued by Pharaoh and his host, he erected on the other side, by divine command, a tabernacle,* which he placed due east and west, to receive the first rays of the rising sun, and to commemorate that mighty east wind by which their miraculous deliverance was effected. This tabernacle was an exact pattern of King Solomon's Temple, of which every Lodge is a representation, and it is, or ought, therefore, to be placed due east and west.

---

* Dr. OLIVER assigns the following reasons why the tabernacle is considered as the type of a Mason's Lodge; "It was an oblong square, and, with its courts and appendages, it represented the whole habitable globe. Such is also the extent of our Lodges. The former was supported by pillars, and the latter is also sustained by those of Wisdom, Strength, and Beauty They were equally situated due east and west. The sacred roll of God's revealed will and law was deposited in the Ark of the Covenant; the same holy record is placed in a conspicuous part of our Lodges. The altar of incense was a double cube, and so is our pedestal and stone of foundation. The covering of the tabernacle was composed of three colors, as a representation of the celestial hemisphere; such, also, is the covering of a Mason's Lodge. The floor of the tabernacle was so holy, that the priests were forbidden to ▓▓▓ upon it without taking off their shoes; the floor of the Lodge is holy ▓▓▓▓▓."

The *orientation* of Lodges, or their position due east and west, is derived from the universal custom of antiquity. "The heathen temples," says DUDLEY, "were so constructed that their length was directed toward the east, and the entrance was by a portico at the western front, where the altar stood, so that the votaries approaching for the performance of religious rites, directed their faces toward the east, the quarter of sunrise." The primitive reason of this custom undoubtedly is to be found in the early prevalence of sun-worship, and hence the spot where that luminary first made his appearance in the heavens was consecrated, in the minds of his worshipers, as a place entitled to peculiar reverence. Long after the reason had ceased, the custom continued to be observed, and Christian churches still are built, when circumstances will permit, with particular reference to an east-and-west position. Freemasonry, retaining in its symbolism the typical reference of the Lodge to the world, and constantly alluding to the sun in his apparent diurnal revolution, imperatively requires, when it can be done, that the Lodge should be situated due east and west, so that every ceremony shall remind the Mason of the progress of that luminary.

Our ancient brethren dedicated their Lodges to King Solomon, because he was our first Most Excellent Grand Master; but modern Masons dedicate theirs to St. John the Baptist and St. John the Evangelist, who were two eminent patrons of Masonry; and since their time, there is represented, in every regular and well-governed Lodge, a certain point within a circle, embordered by two perpendicular parallel lines, representing St. John the Baptist and St. John the Evangelist; and upon the top rests the Holy Scriptures. The point represents an individual brother; the circle is the boundary line, beyond which he is never to suffer his prejudices or passions to betray him. In going round this circle, we neces-

sarily touch upon these two lines, as well as the Holy
Scriptures; and while a Mason keeps himself circumscribed within these due bounds, it is impossible that
he should materially err.

The *point within a circle* is an interesting and important
symbol in Freemasonry, but it has been so debased in the interpretation of it given in the modern lectures, that the sooner that
interpretation is forgotten by the Masonic student, the better
will it be. The symbol is really a beautiful but somewhat
abstruse allusion to the old sun-worship, and introduces us for
the first time to that modification of it known among the ancients
as the worship of the Phallus.

The Phallus was an imitation of the male generative organ.
It was represented usually by a column, which was surrounded
by a circle at its base, intended for the *cteis*, or female generative
organ. This union of the phallus and the cteis, which is well

represented by the *point within the circle*, was intended by the ancients as a type of the prolific powers of nature, which they worshiped under the united form of the active or male principle, and the passive or female principle. Impressed with this idea of the union of these two principles, they made the older of their deities hermaphrodite, and supposed Jupiter, or the Supreme God, to have within himself both sexes, or, as one of their poets expresses it, " to have been created a male and an unpolluted virgin."

Now, this hermaphrodism of the Supreme Divinity was again supposed to be represented by the sun, which was the male generative energy, and by nature or the universe, which was the female prolific principle. And this union was symbolized in different ways, but principally by the *point within the circle*, the point indicating the sun, and the circle the universe of nature, warmed into life by his prolific rays.

The *two parallel lines*, which in the modern lectures are said to represent St. John the Baptist and St. John the Evangelist, really allude to particular periods in the sun's annual course. At two particular points in this course the sun is found on the zodaical signs Cancer and Capricorn, which are distinguished as the summer and winter solstice. When the sun is in these points, he has reached respectively his greatest northern and southern limit. These points, if we suppose the circle to represent the sun's annual course, will be indicated by the points where the parallel lines touch the circle. But the days when the sun reaches these points are the 21st of June and the 22d of December; and this will account for their subsequent application to the two Saints John, whose anniversaries the Church has placed near those days.

So the true interpretation of the point within the circle is the same as that of the Master and Wardens of a Lodge. The reference to the symbolism of the world and the Lodge is preserved in both. The Master and Wardens are symbols of the sun—the Lodge, of the universe or the world ; the point also is the symbol of the same sun, and the surrounding circle of the universe, while the two parallel lines really point, not to two saints, but to the two northern and southern limits of the sun's course

The three great tenets of a Mason's profession are *Brotherly Love, Relief,* and *Truth,* which are thus described :

BROTHERLY LOVE.

By the exercise of brotherly love, we are taught to regard the whole human species as one family ; the high and low the rich and poor ; who, as created by one Almighty Parent, and inhabitants of the same planet, are to aid, support, and protect each other. On this principle, Masonry unites men of every country, sect, and opinion, and conciliates true friendship among those who might otherwise have remained at a perpetual distance.

RELIEF.

To relieve the distressed, is a duty incumbent on all men, but particularly on Masons, who are linked together by an indissoluble chain of sincere affection. To soothe the unhappy, to sympathize with their misfortunes, to compassionate their miseries, and to restore peace to their troubled minds, is the great aim we have in view. On this basis we form our friendships and establish our connections.

TRUTH.

Truth is a divine attribute, and the foundation of every virtue. To be good and true, is the first lesson we are taught in Masonry. On this theme we contemplate, and by its dictates endeavor to regulate our conduct : hence, while influenced by this principle, hypocrisy and deceit are unknown among us, sincerity and plain-dealing distinguish us, and the heart and tongue join in promoting each other's welfare, and rejoicing in each other's prosperity.

Every Mason has four *   *   *   * which are illustrated by the four cardinal virtues, *Temperance, Fortitude, Prudence,* and *Justice,* and are thus explained :

TEMPERANCE.

Temperance is that due restraint upon our affections and passions which renders the body tame and governable, and frees the mind from the allurements of vice. This virtue should be the constant practice of every Mason ; as he is thereby taught to avoid excess, or contracting any licentious or vicious habit, the indulgence of which might lead him to disclose some of those valuable secrets which he has promised to conceal and never reveal, and which would consequently subject him to the contempt and detestation of all good Masons. *   *   *

FORTITUDE.

Fortitude is that noble and steady purpose of the mind whereby we are enabled to undergo any pain, peril, or danger, when prudentially deemed expedient. This virtue is equally distant from rashness and cowardice ; and, like the former, should be deeply impressed upon the mind of every Mason, as a safeguard or security against any illegal attack that may be made, by force or otherwise, to extort from him any of those valuable secrets with which he has been so solemnly intrusted, and which were emblematically represented upon his first admission into the Lodge. * * * *

PRUDENCE.

Prudence teaches us to regulate our lives and actions agreeably to the dictates of reason, and is that habit by which we wisely judge and prudentially determine on all things relative to our present as well as to our future happiness. This virtue should be the peculiar characteristic of every Mason, not only for the government of his conduct while in the Lodge, but also when abroad in the world. It should be particularly attended to in all strange and mixed companies, never to let fall the least sign, token, or word whereby the secrets of Masonry might be unlawfully obtained. * * * *

JUSTICE.

Justice is that standard, or boundary of right, which enables us to render to every man his just due, without distinction. This virtue is not only consistent with Divine and human laws, but is the very cement and support of civil society; and as justice in a great measure constitutes the real good man, so should it be the invariable practice of every Mason never to deviate from the minutest principles thereof. * * * *

As an encouragement and example to the candidate, he is reminded that our ancient brethren served their masters with *freedom*, *fervency*, and *zeal*—which qualities are symbolically illustrated—and the lecture closes with an appropriate reflection on the certainty of death.

CHARGE AT INITIATION INTO THE FIRST DEGREE.*

BROTHER:

As you are now introduced into the first principles of Masonry, I congratulate you on being accepted into this ancient and honorable Order: ancient, as having subsisted from time immemorial; and honorable, as tending, in every particular, so to render all men who will be conformable to its precepts. No institution was ever raised on a better principle or more solid foundation; nor were ever more excellent rules and useful maxims laid down than are inculcated in the several Masonic lectures. The greatest and best of men, in all ages, have been encouragers and promoters of the art, and have never deemed it derogatory to their dignity to level themselves with the fraternity, extend their privileges, and patronize their assemblies. There are three great duties which, as a Mason, you are charged to inculcate—to God, your neighbor, and yourself. To God, in never mentioning his name but with that reverential awe which is due from a creature to his Creator; to implore his aid in all your laudable undertakings, and to esteem him as

* This is a very old charge. The substance of it was written in 1774 by HUTCHINSON, and published in his "Spirit of Masonry." PRESTON considerably enlarged and improved it subsequently, and inserted it in his "Illustrations." WEBB afterward reduced it to its present abridged form, simply by omitting many of PRESTON's paragraphs.

the chief good. To your neighbor, in acting upon the
square, and doing unto him as you wish he should do
unto you. And to yourself, in avoiding all irregu-
larity and intemperance, which may impair your faculties, or debase the dignity of your profession. A
zealous attachment to these duties will insure public
and private esteem.

In the State, you are to be a quiet and peaceful
subject, true to your government, and just to your
country ; you are not to countenance disloyalty or
rebellion, but patiently submit to legal authority, and
conform with cheerfulness to the government of the
country in which you live. In your outward de-
meanor, be particularly careful to avoid censure or
reproach.

Although your frequent appearance at our regular
meetings is earnestly solicited, yet it is not meant
that Masonry should interfere with your necessary
vocations, for these are on no account to be neglected ; neither are you to suffer your zeal for the Institution to lead you into argument with those who,
through ignorance, may ridicule it.

At your leisure hours, that you may improve in
Masonic knowledge, you are to converse with well-
informed brethren, who will be always as ready to
give, as you will be ready to receive, instruction.

Finally, keep sacred and inviolable the mysteries
of the Order, as these are to distinguish you from the
rest of the community, and mark your consequence
among Masons. If, in the circle of your acquaint-
ance, you find a person desirous of being initiated

into Masonry, be particularly attentive not to recommend him unless you are convinced he will conform to our rules ; that the honor, glory, and reputation of the Institution may be firmly established, and the world at large convinced of its good effects.

FELLOW CRAFT'S DEGREE.

SYMBOLISM OF THE DEGREE.

HE symbolism of the second degree essentially differs from that of the first. If the first degree was typical of the period of youth, the second is emblematic of the stage of manhood. Here new duties and increased obligations to their performance press upon the individual. The lessons of wisdom and virtue which he has received in youth, are now to produce their active fruits; the talent which was lent, is now to be returned with usury. Hence, as the Fellow Craft's degree is intended to represent this thinking and working period of life, it necessarily assumes a more important position in the Masonic scale, and is invested with a more dignified ritual, and a more extensive series of instructions. Here it is that the preparatory lessons which were obtained in the first degree are to be enlarged and enforced. As labor is the divinely appointed lot of man, in this degree the rewards of industry are set forth in emblematic forms, and the recipient is taught the exercise of diligence and industry, that by the faithful performance of his task he may, in due time, be entitled to the wages for which he has wrought.

But man was not intended for physical labor only. There are more exalted tasks to which the possession of mind has called him. Endowed by his Creator with the possession of reason and intellect, it is his duty, and should be his pleasure, to direct the vigor and energy of his manhood to the cultivation of his reasoning faculties and the improvement of his intellectual powers.

Hence, the Fellow Craft's degree, as a type of this state of manhood, is particularly devoted to science. The mind of the recipient is fixed, by the nature of its ritual, upon the wonders of nature and art. The attention is particularly directed to the liberal arts and sciences, with whose principles the candidate is charged to become familiar, that he may be enabled to occupy with honor to himself, and with profit to his fellow-creatures, his allotted place in the great structure of human society.

SECOND LECTURE.

The lecture of the second degree is divided into two sections. While it extends the plan of knowledge commenced in the lecture of the first degree, it comprehends a more extensive system of learning, and inculcates, in our peculiar method, the most important truths of science.

FIRST SECTION.

The first section of the second lecture accurately elucidates the mode of initiation into this degree, and instructs the diligent craftsmen how to proceed in the proper arrangement of the ceremonies used on the occasion.

The square, as a symbol, is peculiarly appropriated to this degree. It is intended to teach the Fellow Craft that the square of morality and virtue should be the rule and guide of his conduct in his transactions with all mankind, but more especially with brother Masons.

The following passage of Scripture is introduced during the ceremonies:

Thus he showed me : and, behold, the Lord stood upon a wall made by a plumb-line, with a plumb-line in his hand. And the Lord said unto me, Amos, what seest thou? And I said, A plumb-line. Then said the Lord, Behold, I will set a plumb-line in the midst of my people Israel : I will not again pass by them any more.—*Amos* vii. 7, 8.

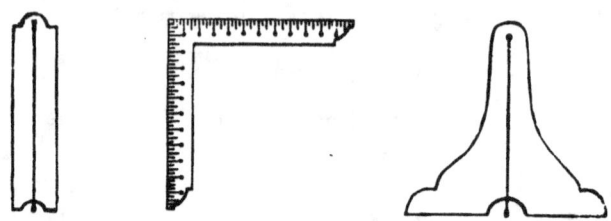

The Working Tools of a Fellow Craft are the *Plumb*, the *Square*, and the *Level*.

The *Plumb* is an instrument made use of by operative masons to raise perpendiculars ; the *Square*, to square their work ; and the *Level*, to lay horizontals ; but we, as Free and Accepted Masons, are taught to make use of them for more noble and glorious purposes : the plumb admonishes us to walk uprightly in our several stations, before God and men, squaring our actions by the square of virtue, and remembering that we are traveling upon the level of time to that undiscovered country from whose bourne no traveler returns.

THE PRECIOUS JEWELS OF A FELLOW CRAFT.

The jewels of a Fellow Craft, like his working tools, and like every other gift that he receives, are altogether of a symbolic nature. They are lessons of instruction which derive their name of jewels from the moral value that they possess. They teach the candidate that the attentive ear receives the sound from the instructive tongue, and the mysteries of Freemasonry are safely lodged in the repository of a faithful breast.

SECOND SECTION.

The second section of this degree refers to the combined operative and speculative origin of the Institution ;* it details some interesting features relative to the Temple of Solomon and the usages of our ancient brethren, in the course of which the mind is drawn to the contemplation of themes of science and philosophy.

* The connection between the operative art and the speculative science of Masonry is the first point to which, in this section, the attention of the candidate is directed. Something ought, therefore, to be here said in reference to these two divisions.

Masonry, in its character as an operative art, is familiar to every one. As such, it is engaged in the application of the rules of architecture to the construction of public and private edifices. It, of course, abounds in the use of technical terms, and makes use of implements and materials which are peculiar to itself. It is the popular theory, that the operative Masons were the founders of the system of speculative Masonry, in which they applied the language and ideas of their art of building to a spiritual and religious sense. Hence Speculative Masonry is nothing more nor less, in this aspect, than a symbolization of Operative Masonry.

The theory is (and it is not an untenable one), that at first operative Masonry existed simply as an art of building. Then the operative Masons, with the assistance of learned and pious men, invented the speculative science, or Freemasonry, and then each became an integrant part of one undivided system. Not, however, that there ever was a time when every operative Mason, without exception, was acquainted with or initiated into the speculative science. Even now there are thousands of skillful stone-masons who know nothing of the symbolic meaning of the implements they employ. But operative Masonry was at first, and is even now, the skeleton upon which was strung the nerves and muscles of the living system of Free or Speculative Masonry.

Speculative Masonry, now known as Freemasonry, is, therefore, the scientific application and the religious consecration of the rules and principles, the technical language and the implements and materials, of operative Masonry to the worship of God as the Grand Architect of the Universe, and to the purification of the heart and the inculcation of the dogmas of a religious philosophy. And as the original union of the operative and speculative branches of the system is traditionally supposed to have taken place at the building of the Temple of Jerusalem by King Solomon, more attention is did in the symbolism to that edifice than to any other.

OPERATIVE MASONRY.

We work in Speculative Masonry, but our ancient brethren wrought in both Operative and Speculative They worked at the building of King Solomon's Tem ple, and many other sacred and important edifices.

By Operative Masonry we allude to a proper appli- cation of the useful rules of architecture, whence a structure will derive figure, strength, and beauty, and whence will result a due proportion and a just corre- spondence in all its parts. It furnishes us with dwellings, and with convenient shelter from the vicis- situdes and inclemencies of the seasons ; and while it displays the effects of human wisdom, as well in the choice as in the arrangement of the sundry materials of which an edifice is composed, it demonstrates that a fund of science and industry is implanted in man for the best, most salutary, and beneficent purposes.

SPECULATIVE MASONRY.

By Speculative Masonry we learn to subdue the passions, act upon the square, keep a tongue of good report, maintain secrecy, and practice charity. It is so far interwoven with religion, as to lay us under obligation to pay that rational homage to the Deity which at once constitutes our duty and our happiness. It leads the contemplative Mason to view, with rev- erence and admiration, the glorious works of creation, and inspires him with the most exalted ideas of the perfections of his Divine Creator.

In six days God created the heavens and the earth, and rested upon the seventh day ; the seventh, there- fore, our ancient brethren consecrated as a day of rest from their labors; thereby enjoying frequent opportunities to contemplate the glorious works of creation, and to adore their great Creator.

THE PILLARS OF THE PORCH.

For he cast two pillars of brass, of eighteen cubits high apiece; and a line of twelve cubits did compass either of them about —1 *Kings* vii. 15.

Also he made before the house two pillars of thirty and five cubits high, and the chapiter that was on the top of each of them was five cubits.—2 *Chron.* iii. 15.

And he made two chapiters of molten brass, to set upon the tops of the pillars: the height of the one chapiter was five cubits, and the height of the other chapiter was five cubits.— 1 *Kings* vii. 16.

The height of the one pillar was eighteen cubits, and the chapiter upon it was brass: and the height of the chapiter three cubits; and the wreathen work, and pomegranates upon the chapiter round about, all of brass: and like unto these had the second pillar with wreathen work.—2 *Kings* xxv. 17.

The discrepancy as to the height of the pillars as given in the book of Kings and in Chronicles is to be reconciled by supposing that in the book of Kings the pillars are spoken of separately, and that in Chronicles their aggregate height is calculated; and the reason that in this latter book their united height is placed at 35 cubits, instead of 36, which would be the double of 18, is because they are there measured as they appear with the chapiters upon them. Now half a cubit of each pillar was concealed in what Dr. Lightfoot calls "the hole of the chapiter," that is, half a cubit's depth of the lower edge of the chapiter covered the top of the pillar, making each pillar apparently only 17½ cubits high, or the two, 35 cubits, as laid down in the book of Chronicles.

In a similar way we reconcile the difference as to the height of the chapiters. In 1 Kings and 2 Chronicles the chapiters are said to be *five* cubits high, while in 2 Kings their height is described as being only *three* cubits. But it will be noticed that it immediately follows in the same place, that "there was a wreathen work and pomegranates upon the chapiter round about." Now this expression is conclusive that the height of the chapiters was estimated exclusive and independent of the wreathen work round about them, which was two cubits more, and this added to the three cubits of the chapiter proper, will make the five cubits spoken of in all other parts of Scripture.*

---

* A cubit was 21 inches. The height of each pillar in English measure was 31 feet 6 inches, and its diameter 7 feet. The height of each chapiter was 8 feet 9 inches, giving a total height of 40 feet 3 inches. The height of the shaft being only four diameters and a half, the pillars bore no resemblance to any of the modern orders of architecture, but were rather an imitation of the massive style of the Egyptians, the lilies on the chapiters being probably an exact copy of the lotus of the Nile, which was a frequent ornamentation among that people.

UNITY, PEACE, AND PLENTY.

Symbols of *Unity, Peace,* and *Plenty* are here introduced and explained.

THE GLOBES.

The globes are two artificial spherical bodies, on the convex surfaces of which are represented the countries, seas, and various parts of the earth. the face of the heavens, the planetary revolutions, and other particulars.

THE USE OF THE GLOBES.

Their principal use, besides serving as maps to distinguish the outward parts of the earth, and the situation of the fixed stars, is to illustrate and explain the phenomena arising from the annual revolution and the diurnal rotation of the earth round its own axis. They are the noblest instruments for improving the mind, and giving it the most distinct idea of any problem or proposition, as well as enabling it to solve the same. Contemplating these bodies, we are inspired with a due reverence for the Deity and his works, and are induced to encourage the studies of astronomy, geography, and navigation, and the arts dependent on them, by which society has been so much benefited.

Reference is here made to the Masonic organization into three degrees—the Entered Apprentice, the Fellow Craft, and the Master Mason—and to its system of government by three officers—the Worshipful Master, the Senior and Junior Wardens.

The five ORDERS OF ARCHITECTURE are next considered.

ORDER IN ARCHITECTURE.

By Order in Architecture is meant a system of all the members, proportions, and ornaments of columns and pilasters; or it is a regular arrangement of the projecting parts of a building, which, united with those of a column, form a beautiful, perfect, and complete whole.

ITS ANTIQUITY.

From the first formation of society, Order in Architecture may be traced. When the rigor of seasons obliged men to contrive shelter from the inclemency of the weather, we learn that they first planted trees on end, and then laid others across, to support a covering. The bands which connected those trees at top and bottom are said to have given rise to the idea of the base and capital of pillars ; and from this simple hint originally proceeded the more improved art of architecture.

The five orders are thus classed : the *Ionic, Doric, Corinthian, Tuscan,* and *Composite.*

THE IONIC

Bears a kind of mean proportion between the more solid and delicate orders. Its column is nine diameters high, its capital is adorned with volutes, and its cornice has dentals. There is both delicacy and ingenuity displayed in this pillar, the invention of which is attributed to the Ionians, as the famous temple of Diana at Ephesus was of this order. It is said to have been formed after the model of an agreeable young woman, of an elegant shape, dressed in her hair, as a contrast to the Doric order, which was formed after that of a strong, robust man.

THE DORIC,

Which is plain and natural, is the most ancient, and was invented by the Greeks. Its column is eight diameters high, and has seldom any ornaments on base or capital, except moldings ; though the frieze is distinguished by triglyphs and metopes, and triglyphs compose the ornaments of the frieze.

The Doric is the best proportioned of all the orders. The several parts of which it is composed are founded on the natural position of solid bodies. In its first invention it was more simple than in its present state. In after times, when it began to be adorned, it gained the name of Doric; for when it was constructed in its primitive and simple form, the name of Tuscan was conferred on it. Hence the Tuscan precedes the Doric in rank, on account of its resemblance to that pillar in its original state.

THE CORINTHIAN,

The richest of the five orders, is deemed a master-piece of art. Its column is ten diameters high, and its capital is adorned with two rows of leaves and eight volutes, which sustain the abacus. The frieze is ornamented with curious devices, the cornice with dentals and modillions. This order is used in stately and superb structures.

THE INVENTION OF THIS ORDER.

It was invented at Corinth, by CALLIMACHUS, who is said to have taken the hint of the capital of this pillar from the following remarkable circumstance. Accidentally passing by the tomb of a young lady, he perceived a basket of toys covered with tile, placed over an acanthus root, having been left there by her nurse. As the branches grew up, they encompassed the basket, till, arriving at the tile, they met with an obstruction, and bent downward. CALLIMACHUS, struck with the object, set about imitating the figure; the vase of the capital he made to represent the basket; the abacus, the tile; and the volutes, the ending leaves.

THE TUSCAN

Is the most simple and solid of the five orders. It was invented in Tuscany, whence it derives its name. Its column is seven diameters high; and its capital, base, and entablature have but few moldings. The simplicity of the construction of this column renders it eligible where ornament would be superfluous.

THE COMPOSITE

Is compounded of the other orders, and was contrived by the Romans. Its capital has the two rows of leaves of the Corinthian, and the volutes of the Ionic. Its column has quarter-rounds, as the Tuscan and Doric orders; is ten diameters high, and its cornice has dentals, or simple modillions. This pillar is generally found in buildings where strength, elegance, and beauty are displayed.

OF THE INVENTION OF ORDER IN ARCHITECTURE.

The ancient and original Orders of Architecture revered by Masons, are no more than three—the Ionic, Doric, and Corinthian, which were invented by the Greeks. To these the Romans have added two: the Tuscan, which they made plainer than the Doric, and the Composite, which was more ornamental, if not more beautiful, than the Corinthian. The first

three orders alone, however, show invention and par
ticular character, and essentially differ from each
other ; the two others have nothing but what is borrowed, and differ only accidentally ; the Tuscan is the
Doric in its earliest state ; and the Composite is the
Corinthian, enriched with the Ionic.   To the Greeks
therefore, and not to the Romans, are we indebted for
what is great, judicious, and distinct in architecture.

Of these five orders, the Ionic, Doric, and Corinthian, as the most ancient, are most esteemed by Masons.
The Ionic, from the skill and ingenuity displayed in
its construction, is emblematic of the column of Wisdom. which is situated in the east part of the Lodge
and is represented by the Worshipful Master ; the
Doric. from the massive strength of its structure is

emblematic of the column of Strength, which is situated in the west part of the Lodge, and is represented by the Senior Warden ; and the Corinthian, from the exuberance of its ornaments, is emblematic of the column of Beauty, which is situated in the south part of the Lodge, and is represented by the Junior Warden.

OF THE SENSES OF HUMAN NATURE.

The five Senses of Human Nature, which are HEARING, SEEING, FEELING, SMELLING, and TASTING, are next referred to and described.

HEARING

Is that sense by which we distinguish sounds, and are capable of enjoying all the agreeable charms of music. By it we are enabled to enjoy the pleasures of society, and reciprocally to communicate to each other our thoughts and intentions, our purposes and desires, while thus our reason is capable of exerting its utmost power and energy.

The wise and beneficent Author of Nature intended, by the formation of this sense, that we should be social creatures, and receive the greatest and most important part of our knowledge by the information of others. For these purposes, we are endowed with hearing, that by a proper exertion of our rational powers, our happiness may be complete.

SEEING

Is that sense by which we distinguish objects, and in an instant of time, without change of place or situation, view armies in battle array, figures of the most stately structures, and all the agreeable variety displayed in the landscape of Nature. By this sense, we find our way on the pathless ocean, traverse the globe of the earth, determine its figure and dimensions, and delineate any region or quarter of it. By it we measure the planetary orbs, and make new discoveries in the sphere of the fixed stars. Nay, more ; by it we perceive the tempers and dispositions, the passions and affections, of our fellow-creatures, when they wish most to conceal them ; so that, though the tongue may be taught to lie and dissemble, the countenance would display the hypocrisy to the discerning eye. In fine, the rays of light which administer to this sense are the most astonishing part of the animated creation, and render the eye a peculiar object of admiration.

Of all the faculties, sight is the noblest. The structure of the eye and its appurtenances evince the admirable contrivance of Nature for performing all its various external and internal motions, while the variety displayed in the eyes of different animals, suited to their several ways of life, clearly demonstrates this organ to be the master-piece of Nature's work.

FEELING

Is that sense by which we distinguish the different qualities of bodies, such as heat and cold, hardness and softness, roughness and smoothness, figure, solidity, motion, and extension.

SMELLING

Is that sense by which we distinguish odors, the various kinds of which convey different impressions to the mind. Animal and vegetable bodies, and, indeed, most other bodies, while exposed to the air, continually send forth effluvia of vast subtilty, as well in the state of life and growth, as in the state of fermentation and putrefaction. These effluvia being drawn into the nostrils along with the air, are the means by which all bodies are smelled. Hence it is evident that there is a manifest appearance of design in the great Creator's having planted the organ of smell in the inside of that canal through which the air continually passes in respiration.

TASTING

Enables us to make a proper distinction in the choice of our food. The organ of this sense guards the entrance of the alimentary canal, as that of smelling guards the entrance of the canal for respiration. From the situation of both these organs, it is plain that they were intended by Nature to distinguish wholesome food from that which is nauseous. Everything that enters into the stomach must undergo the scrutiny of tasting; and by it we are capable of discerning the changes which the same body undergoes in the different compositions of art, cookery, chemistry, pharmacy, etc.

Smelling and tasting are inseparably connected; and it is by the unnatural kind of life men commonly lead in society, that these senses are rendered less fit to perform their natural offices.

Of these senses, *Hearing*, *Seeing*, and *Feeling* have always been highly revered by Masons. * * * *

The seven Liberal Arts and Sciences—which are GRAMMAR, RHETORIC, LOGIC, ARITHMETIC, GEOMETRY, MUSIC, and ASTRONOMY—are then described.

GRAMMAR

Teaches the proper arrangement of words, according to the idiom or dialect of any particular people ; and that excellency of pronunciation which enables us to speak or write a language with accuracy, agreeably to reason and correct usage.

RHETORIC

Teaches us to speak copiously and fluently on any subject, not merely with propriety alone, but with all the advantages of force and elegance, wisely contriving to captivate the hearer by strength of argument and beauty of expression, whether it be to entreat or exhort, to admonish or applaud.

LOGIC

Teaches us to guide our reason discretionally in the general knowledge of things, and directs our inquiries after truth. It consists of a regular train of argument, whence we infer, deduce, and conclude, according to certain premises laid down, admitted, or granted ; and in it are employed the faculties of conceiving, judging, reasoning, and disposing, all of which are naturally led on from one gradation to another, till the point in question is finally determined.

This science ought to be cultivated as the foundation, or ground-work, of our inquiries ; particularly in the pursuit of those sublime principles which claim our attention as Masons.

ARITHMETIC

Teaches the powers and properties of numbers, which are variously effected, by letters, tables, figures, and instruments. By this art, reasons and demonstrations are given for finding out any certain number whose relation or affinity to another is already known or discovered. The greater advancement we make in the mathematical sciences, the more capable we shall be of considering such things as are the ordinary objects of our conceptions, and be thereby led to a more comprehensive knowledge of our great Creator and the works of the creation.

GEOMETRY

Treats of the powers and properties of magnitudes in general, where length, breadth, and thickness are considered, from a point to a line, from a line to a superficies, and from a superficies to a solid.

A point is a dimensionless figure, or an indivisible part of a space.

A line is a point continued, and a figure of one capacity, namely, length.

A superficies is a figure of two dimensions, namely, length and breadth.

A solid is a figure of three dimensions, namely, length, breadth, and thickness.

THE ADVANTAGES OF GEOMETRY.

By this science the architect is enabled to construct his plans and execute his designs; the general, to arrange his soldiers; the geographer, to give us the dimensions of the world, and all things therein contained ; to delineate the extent of seas, and specify the divisions of empires, kingdoms, and provinces. By it, also, the astronomer is enabled to make his observations, and to fix the duration of time and seasons, years and cycles.

In fine, geometry is the foundation of architecture, and the root of the mathematics.

MUSIC

Teaches the art of forming concords, so as to compose delightful harmony, by a mathematical and proportional arrangement of acute, grave, and mixed sounds. This art, by a series of experiments, is reduced to a demonstrative science, with respect to tones and the intervals of sound. It inquires into the nature of concords and discords, and enables us to find out the proportion between them by numbers.

ASTRONOMY

Is that divine art by which we are taught to read the wisdom, strength, and beauty of the Almighty Creator in those sacred pages, the celestial hemisphere.

Assisted by astronomy, we can observe the magnitudes, and calculate the periods and eclipses of the heavenly bodies. By it we learn the use of the globes, the system of the world, and the preliminary laws of nature. While we are employed in the study of this science, we must perceive unparalleled instances of wisdom and goodness ; and, through the whole creation, trace the glorious Author by his works.

Here a symbol of Plenty is introduced, and proper explanations are given as to the proper answers to the following questions:

What does it denote?

How was it represented?

Why was it instituted?

The passages of Scripture which are referred to in this part of the section will be found in Judges xii. 1–6. The Vulgate version gives a paraphrastic translation of a part of the 6th verse, as follows: "Say, therefore, Shibboleth, which being interpreted is an *ear of corn*." The same word also in Hebrew signifies a rapid stream of water, from the root SHaBaL, to flow copiously. The too common error of speaking, in this part of the ritual, of a "*water-ford*" instead of a "*water-fall*," which is the correct word, must be carefully avoided. A *water-fall* is an emblem of plenty, because it indicates an abundance of water. A *water-ford*, for the converse reason, is, if any symbol at all, a symbol of scarcity.

The lecture next proceeds to illustrate

THE MORAL ADVANTAGES OF GEOMETRY.

Geometry, the first and noblest of sciences, is the basis on which the superstructure of Masonry is erected. By geometry, we may curiously trace Nature, through her various windings, to her most concealed recesses. By it we may discover the power, the wisdom, and the goodness of the Grand Artificer of the Universe, and view with delight the proportions which connect this vast machine.

By it we may discover how the planets move in their different orbits, and demonstrate their various revolutions. By it we account for the return of seasons, and the variety of scenes which each season displays to the discerning eye. Numberless worlds are around us, all framed by the same Divine Artist, which roll through the vast expanse, and are all conducted by the same unerring law of Nature.

A survey of Nature, and the observations of her beautiful proportions, first determined man to imitate the Divine plan, and study symmetry and order. This gave rise to societies, and birth to every useful art. The architect began to design, and the plans which he laid down, being improved by experience and time, have produced works which are the admiration of every age.

The lapse of time, the ruthless hand of ignorance, and the devastations of war, have laid waste and destroyed many valuable monuments of antiquity on which the utmost exertions of human genius have been employed. Even the Temple of Solomon, so spacious and magnificent, and constructed by so many celebrated artists, escaped not the unsparing ravages of barbarous force. Freemasonry, notwithstanding, has still survived. The *attentive ear* receives the sound from the *instructive tongue*, and the mysteries of Freemasonry are safely lodged in the repository of *faithful breasts*. Tools and instruments of architecture, and symbolic emblems, most expressive, are selected by the fraternity to imprint on the mind wise and serious truths; and thus, through a succession of ages, are transmitted, unimpaired, the most excellent tenets of our institution.*

The lecture closes by paying profound homage to the sacred name of the Grand Geometrician of the Universe, before whom all Masons, from the youngest E∴ A∴ who stands in the northeast corner of the Lodge, to the W∴ M∴ who presides in the east, humbly, reverently, and devoutly bow.

————◆◆◆————

CHARGE AT PASSING TO THE DEGREE OF FELLOW CRAFT.†
BROTHER:

Being passed to the second degree of Masonry, we congratulate you on your preferment. The internal, and not the external, qualifications of a man are what Masonry regards. As you increase in knowledge, you will improve in social intercourse.

It is unnecessary to recapitulate the duties which as a Mason, you are bound to discharge, or to enlarge on the necessity of a strict adherence to them, as your own experience must have established their value. Our laws and regulations you are strenuously to support, and be always ready to assist in seeing them duly executed. You are not to palliate or aggravate

* This descant on geometry is, perhaps, one of the oldest passages in our monitorial instruction. It originally constituted a part of an address, entitled "A Vindication of Masonry," delivered on the 15th May, 1741, by Brother CHARLES LESLIE, before Vernon Kilwinning Lodge, in the city of Edinburgh.

† This charge is taken, with but very little alteration, from WILLIAM PRESTON, who first published it in his "Illustrations of Masonry."

the offenses of your brethren ; but in the decision of every trespass against our rules, you are to judge with candor, admonish with friendship, and reprehend with justice.

The study of the liberal arts, that valuable branch of education which tends so effectually to polish and adorn the mind, is earnestly recommended to your consideration ; especially the science of geometry, which is established as the basis of our art. Geometry, or Masonry, originally synonymous terms, being of a divine and moral nature, is enriched with the most useful knowledge ; while it proves the wonderful properties of nature, it demonstrates the more important truths of morality.

Your past behavior and regular deportment have merited the honor which we have now conferred ; and in your new character it is expected that you will conform to the principles of the Order, by steadily persevering in the practice of every commendable virtue. Such is the nature of your engagement as a Fellow Craft, and to these duties you are bound by the most sacred ties.

LECTURE ON THE WINDING STAIRS.

Having passed through the Winding Stairs to the Middle Chamber, it is proper that you should be made acquainted with the symbolic meaning of the ceremonies in which you have been engaged.

Although the legend of the Winding Stairs forms an important tradition of Ancient Craft Masonry, the only allusion to it in Scripture is to be found in a single verse in the 6th chapter of the 1st Book of Kings, and is in these words: "The door for the middle chamber was in the right side of the house; and they went up with winding stairs into the middle chamber, and out of the middle into the third." Out of this slender material has been constructed an allegory, which, if properly considered in its symbolical relations, will be found to be of surpassing beauty. But it is only as a symbol that we can regard this whole tradition, for the historical facts and the architectural details alike forbid us for a moment to suppose that the legend, as it is rehearsed in the second degree of Masonry, is anything more than a magnificent philosophical myth.

Let us inquire into the true design of this legend, and learn the lesson of symbolism which it is intended to teach.

In the investigation of the true meaning of every Masonic symbol and allegory, we must be governed by the single principle that the whole design of Freemasonry as a speculative science is the investigation of divine truth. To this great object everything is subsidiary. The Mason is, from the moment of his initiation as an Entered Apprentice, to the time at which he receives the full fruition of Masonic light, an investigator—a laborer in the quarry and the Temple—whose reward is to be Truth, and all the ceremonies and traditions of the Order tend to this ultimate design.

Hence there is in Speculative Masonry always a progress, symbolized by its peculiar ceremonies of initiation. There is an advancement from a lower to a higher state—from darkness to light—from death to life—from error to truth. The candidate is always ascending; he is never stationary; never goes back; but each step he takes brings him to some new mental illumination—to the knowledge of some more elevated doctrine. The teaching of the Divine Master is, in respect to this continual progress, the teaching of Masonry—"No man having put his hand to the plow, and looking back, is fit for the kingdom of heaven." And similar to this is the precept of PYTHAGORAS: "When traveling, turn not back, for if you do, the furies will accompany you."

In an investigation of the symbolism of the Winding Stairs, we will be directed to the true explanation by a reference to their origin, their number, the objects which they recall, and their termination; but, above all, by a consideration of the great design which an ascent upon them was intended to accomplish.

The steps of this winding staircase commenced, we are in-formed, at the porch of the Temple—that is to say, at its very entrance. But nothing is more undoubted in the science of Masonic symbolism than that the Temple was the representative of the world, purified by the Shekinah, or the Divine Presence. The world of the profane is without the Temple; the world of the initiated is within its sacred walls. Hence, to enter the temple, to pass within the porch, to be made a Mason, and to be born into the world of Masonic light, are all synonymous and convertible terms. Here, then, the symbolism of the Winding Stairs begins.

The Apprentice, having entered within the porch of the temple, has begun his Masonic life. But the first degree in Masonry, like the lesser mysteries of the ancient systems of initiation, is only a preparation and purification for something higher. The Entered Apprentice is the child in Masonry. The lessons which he receives are simply intended to cleanse the heart and prepare the recipient for that mental illumination which is to be given in the succeeding degrees.

As a Fellow Craft, he has advanced another step, and as the degree is emblematic of youth, so it is here that the intellectual education of the candidate begins. And therefore, here, at the very spot which separates the Porch from the Sanctuary, where childhood ends and manhood begins, he finds stretching out before him a winding stair which invites him, as it were, to ascend, and which, as the symbol of discipline and instruction, teaches him that here must commence his Masonic labor—here he must enter upon those glorious, though difficult researches, the end of which is to be the possession of divine truth. The Winding Stairs begin after the candidate has passed within the Porch and between the pillars of Strength and Establishment, as a significant symbol to teach him that as soon as he had passed beyond the years of irrational childhood, and commenced his entrance upon manly life, the laborious task of self-improve-ment is the first duty that is placed before him. He can not stand still, if he would be worthy of his vocation; his destiny as an immortal being requires him to ascend, step by step, until he has reached the summit, where the treasures of knowledge await him.

The candidate, then, in the second degree of Masonry, represents a man starting forth on the journey of life, with the great task before him of self-improvement. For the faithful performance of this task, a reward is promised, which reward consists in the development of all his intellectual faculties, the moral and spiritual elevation of his character, and the acquisition of truth and knowledge. Now, the attainment of this moral and intellectual condition supposes an elevation of character, an ascent from a lower to a higher life, and a passage of toil and difficulty. through rudimentary instruction, to the full fruition of wisdom. This is therefore beautifully symbolized by the Winding Stairs, at whose foot the aspirant stands ready to climb the toilsome steep, while at its top is placed "that hieroglyphic bright, which none but Craftsmen ever saw," as the emblem of divine truth. And hence a distinguished writer has said that " these steps, like all the Masonic symbols, are illustrative of discipline and doctrine, as well as of natural, mathematical, and metaphysical science, and open to us an extensive range of moral and speculative inquiry."

The candidate, incited by the love of virtue and the desire of knowledge, and withal eager for the reward of truth which is set before him, begins at once the toilsome ascent. At each division he pauses to gather instruction from the symbolism which these divisions present to his attention.

At the first pause which he makes, he is instructed in th- peculiar organization of the Order of which he has become a disciple. But the information here given, if taken in its naked, literal sense, is barren, and unworthy of his labor. The rank of the officers who govern, and the names of the degrees which constitute the institution, can give him no knowledge which he has not before possessed. We must look, therefore, to the symbolic meaning of these allusions for any value which may be attached to this part of the ceremony.

The reference to the organization of the Masonic institution is intended to remind the aspirant of the union of men in society and the development of the social state out of the state of nature. He is thus reminded, in the very outset of his journey, of the blessings which arise from civilization, and of the fruits of virtue and knowledge which are derived from that condition. Masonry itself is the result of civilization; while in grateful return it has been one of the most important means of extending that condition of mankind.

All the monuments of antiquity that the ravages of time have left, combine to prove that man had no sooner emerged from the savage into the social state, than he commenced the organization of religious mysteries, and the separation, by a sort of divine instinct, of the sacred from the profane. Then came the invention of architecture as a means of providing convenient dwellings and necessary shelter from the inclemencies and vicissitudes of the seasons, with all the mechanical arts connected with it, and lastly, geometry, as a necessary science to enable the cultivators of land to measure and designate the limits of their possessions. All these are claimed as peculiar characteristics of Speculative Masonry, which may be considered as the type of civilization, the former bearing the same relation to the profane world as the latter does to the savage state. Hence, we at once see the fitness of the symbolism which commences the aspirant's upward progress in the cultivation of knowledge and the search after truth, by recalling to his mind the condition of civilization and the social union of mankind, as necessary preparations for the attainment of these objects. In the allusions to the officers of a Lodge, and the degrees of Masonry as explanatory of the organization of our own society, we clothe in our symbolic language the history of the organization of society.

Advancing in his progress, the candidate is invited to contemplate another series of instructions. The Human Senses, as the appropriate channels through which we receive all our ideas of perception, and which, therefore, constitute the most important sources of our knowledge, are here referred to as a symbol of intellectual cultivation. Architecture, as the most important of the arts which conduce to the comfort of mankind, is also alluded to here, not simply because it is so closely connected with the operative institution of Masonry, but also as the type of all the other useful arts. In his second pause, in the ascent of the Winding Stairs, the aspirant is therefore reminded of the necessity of cultivating practical knowledge.

So far, then, the instructions he has received relate to his own condition in society, as a member of the great social compact, and to his means of becoming, by a knowledge of the arts of practical life, a necessary and useful member of that society.

But his motto will be, "Onward and forward!" The stair is still before him; its summit is not yet reached, and still further treasures of wisdom are to be sought for, or the reward will not be gained, nor the *middle chamber*, the abiding-place of truth, be reached.

In his third pause, he therefore arrives at that point in which the whole circle of human science is to be explained. Symbols are in themselves arbitrary and of conventional signification, and the complete circle of human science might have been as well symbolized by any other sign or series of doctrines as by the seven liberal Arts and Sciences. But Masonry is an institution of the olden time; and this selection of the liberal arts and sciences as a symbol of the completion of human learning is one of the most pregnant evidences that we have of its antiquity.

In the seventh century, and for a long time afterward, the circle of instruction to which all the learning of the most eminent schools and most distinguished philosophers was confined, was limited to what was then called the liberal arts and sciences, and consisted of two branches, the *trivium* and the *quadrivium*.* The *trivium* included grammar, rhetoric, and logic; the *quadrivium* comprehended arithmetic, geometry, music, and astronomy.

These seven heads were supposed to include universal knowledge. He who was master of these was thought to have no need of a preceptor to explain any books or to solve any questions which lay within the compass of human reason; the knowledge of the *trivium* having furnished him with the key to

---

* The words themselves are purely classical, but the meanings here given to them are of a mediæval or corrupt Latinity. Among the old Romans, a *trivium* meant a place where three ways met, and a *quadrivium*, where four, or what we now call a *cross-road*. When we speak of the *paths of learning*, we readily discover the origin of the signification given by the scholastic philosophers to these terms.

all language, and that of the *quadrivium* having opened to him the secret laws of Nature.

At a period when few were instructed in the *trivium*, and very few studied the *quadrivium*, to be master of both was sufficient to complete the character of a philosopher. The propriety, therefore, of adopting the seven liberal Arts and Sciences as a symbol of the completion of human learning is apparent. The candidate, having reached this point, is now supposed to have accomplished the task upon which he had entered—he has reached the last step, and is now ready to receive the full fruition of human learning.

So far, then, we are able to comprehend the true symbolism of the Winding Stairs. They represent the progress of an inquiring mind with the toils and labors of intellectual cultivation and study, and the preparatory acquisition of all human science, as a preliminary step to the attainment of divine truth, which it must be remembered is always symbolized in Masonry by the WORD.

Here we may allude to the symbolism of numbers, which is for the first time presented to the consideration of the Masonic student, in the legend of the Winding Stairs. The theory of numbers as the symbols of certain qualities was originally borrowed by the Masons from the school of PYTHAGORAS. According to that system, the fact that the total number of the steps amount in all to *fifteen*, is a significant symbol. For *fifteen* was a sacred number among the Orientals, because the letters of the holy name, JAH, were, in their numerical value, equivalent to fifteen; and hence a figure, in which the nine digits were so disposed as to make fifteen either way when added together perpendicularly, horizontally, or diagonally, constituted one of their most sacred talismans. The fifteen steps in the Winding Stairs are therefore symbolic of the name of God.

But we are not yet done. It will be remembered that a reward was promised for all this toilsome ascent of the Winding Stairs. Now, what are the wages of a Speculative Mason? Not money, nor wine, nor oil. All these are but symbols. His wages are truth, or that approximation to it which will be most appropriate to the degree into which he has been initiated. It is one of the most beautiful, but at the same time most abstruse, doctrines of the science of Masonic symbolism, that the Mason is ever to be in search of truth, but is never to find it. And this is intended to teach the humiliating but necessary lesson, that the knowledge of the nature of God and of man's relation to him, which knowledge constitutes divine truth, can never be acquired in this life. It is only when the portals of the grave open to us, and give us an entrance into a more perfect life, that this knowledge is to be attained.

The Middle Chamber is, therefore, symbolic of this life, where only the symbol of the word can be given, where only the truth is to be reached by approximation, and yet where we are to learn that that truth will consist in a perfect knowledge of the G. A. O. T. U. This is the reward of the inquiring Mason; in this consists the wages of a Fellow Craft; he is directed to the truth, but must travel farther and ascend still higher to attain it.

It is, then, as a symbol, and a symbol only, that we must study this beautiful legend of the Winding Stairs. If we attempt to adopt it as a historical fact, the absurdity of its details stares us in the face, and wise men will wonder at our credulity. Its inventors had no desire thus to impose upon our folly; but offering it to us as a great philosophical myth, they did not for a moment suppose that we would pass over its sublime moral teachings to accept the allegory as a historical narrative, without meaning, and wholly irreconcilable with the records of Scripture, and opposed by all the principles of probability. To suppose that eighty thousand craftsmen were weekly paid in the narrow precincts of the Temple chambers, is simply to suppose an absurdity. But to believe that all this pictorial representation of an ascent by a Winding Staircase to the place where the wages of labor were to be received, was an allegory to teach us the ascent of the mind from ignorance, through all the toils of study and the difficulties of obtaining knowledge, receiving here a little and there a little, adding something to the stock of our ideas at each step, until, in the middle chamber of life— in the full fruition of manhood—the reward is attained, and the purified and elevated intellect is invested with the reward, in the direction how to seek God and God's truth—to believe this, is to believe and to know the true design of Speculative Masonry, the only design which makes it worthy of a good or a wise man's study.

Its historical details are barren, but its symbols and allegories are fertile with instruction.

And so we close with this lesson: *The Fellow Craft represents a man laboring in the pursuit of truth; and the Winding Stairs are the devious pathways of that pursuit.*

MASTER MASON'S DEGREE.

SYMBOLISM OF THE DEGREE.

F the first degree is intended as a representation of youth, and the second of manhood, the third, or MASTER MASON, is emblematic of old age, with its trials, its sufferings,
and its final termination in death. The time for
toiling is now over; the opportunity to learn
has passed away; the spiritual temple that we
all have been striving to erect in our hearts is
now nearly completed, and the wearied workman awaits only the word of the Grand Master
of the Universe, to call him from the labors
of earth to the eternal refreshments of heaven.
Hence, this is by far the most solemn and impressive of the degrees of Masonry; and it has, in consequence of the profound
truths which it inculcates, been distinguished by the craft as the
sublime degree. As an Entered Apprentice, the Mason was
taught those elementary instructions which were to fit him for
further advancement in his profession, just as the youth is supplied with that rudimentary education which is to prepare him

for entering on the active duties of life; as a Fellow Craft, the Mason is directed to continue his investigations in the science of the Institution, and to labor diligently in the tasks it pre scribes, just as the man is required to enlarge his mind by the acquisition of new ideas, and to extend his usefulness to his fel low-creatures; but, as a Master, the Mason is taught the last, the most important, and the most necessary of truths, that hav ir g been faithful to all his trusts, he is at last to die, and to re ceive the rewards of his fidelity.

It was the single object of all the ancient rites and mysteries practiced in the very bosom of pagan darkness, shining as a sol itary beacon in all that surrounding gloom, and cheering the philosopher in his weary pilgrimage of life, to teach the immor tality of the soul. This is still the great design of the third degree of Masonry. This is the scope and aim of its ritual. The Master Mason represents man, when youth, manhood, old age, and life itself have passed away as fleeting shadows, yet raised from the grave of iniquity, and quickened into another and a better existence. By its legend and all its ritual, it is implied that we have been redeemed from the death of sin and the sepul chre of pollution. "The ceremonies and the lecture," as a dis tinguished writer has observed, "beautifully illustrate this all-engrossing subject; and the conclusion we arrive at is, that youth, properly directed, leads us to honorable and virtuous maturity, and that the life of man, regulated by morality, faith, and justice, will be rewarded at its closing hour by the prospect of eternal bliss."

THIRD LECTURE.

This has very properly been called the *sublime degree of a Master Mason*, as well for the solemnity of the ceremonies which accompany it, as for the profound lessons of wisdom which it inculcates. The important design of the degree is to symbolize the great doctrines of the resurrection of the body and the immortality of the soul; and hence it has been remarked by a learned writer of our Order, that the Master Mason repre sents a man saved from the grave of iniquity, and raised to the faith of salvation. The lecture is divided into three sections.

FIRST SECTION.

The ceremony of raising a candidate to the sublime degree of a Master Mason is particularly described in the first section, which, though brief, will be found essentially useful.

The Compasses are peculiarly consecrated to this degree, because within their extreme points, when properly extended, are emblematically said to be inclosed the principal tenets of our profession, and hence the moral application of the Compasses, in the third degree, is to those precious jewels of a Master Mason, Friendship, Morality, and Brotherly Love.

The following passage of Scripture is introduced during the ceremonies :

Remember now thy Creator in the days of thy youth, while the evil days come not, nor the years draw nigh, when thou shalt say, I have no pleasure in them ; while the sun, or the light, or the moon, or the stars, be not darkened, nor the clouds return after the rain : in the day when the keepers of the house shall tremble, and the strong men shall bow themselves, and the grinders cease because they are few, and those that look out of the windows be darkened, and the doors shall be shut in the streets when the sound of the grinding is low, and he shall rise up at the voice of the bird, and all the daughters of music shall be brought low ; also when they shall be afraid of that which is high, and fears shall be in the way, and the almond tree shall flourish, and the grasshopper shall be a burden. and desire shall fail : **because man** goeth to his long home, and the mourners go about the streets : or ever the silver cord be loosed, or the golden bowl be broken, or the pitcher be broken at the fountain, or the wheel broken at the cistern.   Then shall the dust return to the earth as it was   and the spirit shall return unto God who gave it.—*Ecclesiastes* xii. 1-7.

The passage of Scripture here selected is a beautiful and affecting description of the body of man suffering under the infirmities of old age, and metaphorically compared to a worn-out house about to fall into decay.   How appropriate is such an introduction to the sublime and awful ceremonies of that degree, in which death, the resurrection, and life eternal are the lessons to be taught by all its symbols and allegories !

The *Working Tools* of a Master Mason are all the implements of masonry indiscriminately, but more especially the *Trowel*.

The *Trowel* is an instrument made use of by Operative Masons, to spread the cement which unites a building into one common mass ; but we, as Free and Accepted Masons, are taught to make use of it for the more noble and glorious purpose of spreading the cement of brotherly love and affection ; that cement which unites us into one sacred band, or society of friends and brothers, among whom no contention should ever exist, but that noble contention, or rather emulation, of who can best work and best agree.

The three *precious jewels* of a Master Mason are here referred to

SECOND SECTION.

The second section of this lecture is of pre-eminent importance. It recites the legend or historical tradition on which the degree is founded ; a legend whose symbolic interpretation testifies our faith in the resurrection of the body and the immortality of the soul, while it exemplifies a rare instance of virtue, fortitude, and integrity.

The legend of the third degree has been considered of so much importance that it has been preserved in the symbolism of every Masonic rite. No matter what modifications or alterations the general system may have undergone—no matter how much the ingenuity or the imagination of the founders of rites may have perverted or corrupted other symbols, abolishing the old, and substituting new ones—the legend of the Temple Builder has ever been left untouched, to present itself in all the integrity of its ancient mythical form.

The idea of the legend was undoubtedly borrowed from the Ancient Mysteries, where the lesson was the same as that now conveyed in the third degree of Masonry.

Viewed in this light, it is evident that it is not essential to the value of the symbolism that the legend should be proved to be historical. Whether considered as a truthful narrative of an event that actually transpired during the building of the Temple, or simply as a myth, embodying the utterance of a religious sentiment, the symbolic lesson of life and death and immortality is still contained in its teachings, and commands our earnest attention.

Again is the lesson taught here, as it was in the first degree, that a Mason should enter upon no great and important labor without first invoking the blessing of Deity. But the symbolism here is still further extended, and the candidate, representing one who is about to enter upon the pilgrimage of life, and all its dangers and temptations, first is supposed to lay down upon his trestle-board the designs of labor, of honest ambition, or of virtuous pleasure upon which he is about to enter, and then to invoke the protection and blessing of the Grand Architect of the Universe upon his future career. For the Temple Builder is, in the Masonic system, the symbol of humanity developed here and in the life to come; and as the Temple is the visible symbol of the world, its architect becomes the mythical symbol of man, the dweller and worker in the world, and his progress by the gates is the allegory of man's pilgrimage through youth, manhood, and old age, to the final triumph of death and the grave.

The number 12 was celebrated as a mystical number in the ancient systems of sun-worship, of which it has already been said that Masonry is a philosophical development. The number there referred to the twelve signs of the zodiac, and in those Masonic rites in which the Builder is made the symbol of the sun, the twelve F∴ C∴ refer to the twelve signs in which alone the sun is to be sought for. But in the York rite this symbolism is lost, because HIRAM there represents man, and not the sun. But the ancient number has still been preserved. PORTAL says the number *twelve* was a perfect and complete number. The number thirteen indicated the commencement of a new course of life, and thence it became the emblem of death. The number twelve has always been considered as a sacred number: witness the 12 great gods of the Greeks and Romans; the 12 altars of Janus, referring to the 12 months of the year, the 12 tribes of Israel, the 12 Apostles, and a hundred other instances that, if necessary, might be cited.

A WAYFARING MAN.—The word means a traveler, one who passes over the road—derived from *way* or road, and the word *fare*, in its old meaning of to *pass or go over*. BAILEY defines a wayfaring man as "one who is accustomed to travel over the roads." It is with this meaning frequently found in Scripture, as in Judges xix. 17: "And when he had lifted up his eyes, he saw a wayfaring man in the street of the city." Such a man, having perhaps just landed at Joppa, and on his way to the interior, would be most likely to be met near that city, and would be best enabled to give any information wanted as to the condition of the shipping in the harbor, or in relation to any other matter connected with a passage.

The word "*sea-faring man*," sometimes ignorantly used in this place, is a monstrous corruption of the old term.

Joppa, which was by the Hebrews called Japho, and is now known as Jaffa, was and is a sea-port town and harbor on the coast of Palestine, about forty miles in "a westerly direction" (being about northwest) from Jerusalem. At the time of the building of the Temple it was the only sea-port possessed by the

Israelites, and was therefore the point through which all passage out of or into the country was effected.

The *small hill near* Mount Moriah can be clearly identified by the most convincing analogies as being no other than Mount Calvary. Thus Mount Calvary was a *small hill ;* it was situated in a *westerly direction* from the Temple, and near Mount Moriah ; it was on the direct road from Jerusalem to Joppa, and is thus the very spot where a *weary brother*, traveling on that road, would find it convenient *to sit down to rest and refresh himself ;* it was outside of the gate of the Temple ; and lastly, there are several caves, or *clefts in the rocks*, in the neighbor hood, one of which, it will be remembered, was, subsequently to the time of this tradition, used as the sepulchre of our Lord. The Christian Mason will readily perceive the peculiar character of the symbolism which this identification of the spot on which the great truth of the resurrection was unfolded in both systems—the Masonic and the Christian—must suggest.

The *Sprig of Acacia* is an important symbol in Freemasonry. The plant is known to botanists as the *acacia vera* of TOURNE FORT and the *mimosa nilotica* of LINNÆUS. It is an evergreen that grows in great abundance in the vicinity of Jerusalem. Its name in Hebrew is *Shittah*, or in the plural, *Shittim*, and it was always esteemed as a sacred tree by the Israelites. The taber nacle and its furniture, with the Ark of the Covenant, was made out of it, and it was consecrated, from among the other trees of the forest, to sacred purposes.

As a symbol, it received, among the ancients, three interpretations. 1. In consequence of its incorruptible and evergreen nature, it was readily adopted as a symbol of the IMMORTALITY OF THE SOUL. 2. In allusion to the derivation of its name, among the Greeks, from a word which signifies *freedom from sin*, it was also adopted as a symbol of INNOCENCE. 3. Like all the other sacred plants, such as the myrtle, the mistletoe, and the lotus, which were used in the Ancient Mysteries, it became a symbol of INITIATION. The three interpretations combined teach us, by the use of this one symbol, that in the *initiation* of life and death, of which the initiation in the third degree is simply emblematic, *innocence* must for a time lie in the grave—at length, however, to be called by the Grand Master of all things to *immortality*.

CLEFTS IN THE ROCKS.—The vicinity of Jerusalem is exceeding rocky and mountainous. These rocks abound in clefts or caves, which were sometimes used by the inhabitants as places of sepulture, sometimes as places of refuge in time of war, and sometimes as lurking-places for robbers, or for *persons guilty of crime and fleeing from justice*.

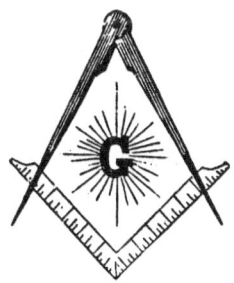

THE GRAND MASTER'S JEWEL.—There is a Masonic tradition, that the Jewel of an ancient Grand Master—and the one therefore always worn by the Builder—was the Square and Compasses, with the letter G between. The finding of this jewel alone gives any probability to this part of the legend.

It is hardly necessary to say that the letter G, wherever

spoken of in Masonry as a symbol, is merely a modern substitute for the Hebrew letter *yod*, י, which was the initial of *Jehovah*, the tetragammaton, and therefore constantly used as a symbol of Deity.

The following DIRGE is sung:

Solemn strikes the funeral chime—
Notes of our departing time,
As we journey here below,
Through a pilgrimage of woe.

Mortals, now indulge a tear,
For Mortality is here!
See how wide her trophies wave
O'er the slumbers of the grave!

Calm, the good man meets his fate,
Guards celestial 'round him wait!
See! he bursts these mortal chains,
And o'er death the victory gains,

Here another guest we bring--
Seraphs of celestial wing,
To our funeral altar come,
Waft this friend and brother home

There, enlarged, thy soul shall see
What was vailed in mystery;
Heavenly glories of the place
Show his Maker face to face.

Lord of all! below—above—
Fill our hearts with truth and love;
When dissolves our earthly tie,
Take us to thy Lodge on high.

Prayer at raising a brother to the sublime degree of Master Mason.

Thou, O God! knowest our down-sitting and our up-rising, and understandest our thoughts afar off. Shield and defend us from the evil intentions of our enemies, and support us under the trials and afflictions we are destined to endure, while traveling through this vale of tears. Man, that is born of a woman, is of few days, and full of trouble. He cometh forth as a flower, and is cut down; he fleeth also as a shadow, and continueth not. Seeing his days are determined, the number of his months are with thee; thou hast appointed his bounds that he can not pass; turn from him that he may rest, till he shall accomplish his day. For there is hope of a tree if it be cut down, that it will sprout again, and that the tender branch thereof will not cease. But man dieth and wasteth away; yea, man giveth up the ghost, and where is he? As the waters fail from the sea, and the flood decayeth and drieth up, so man lieth down and riseth not up, till the heavens shall be no more. Yet, O Lord! have compassion on the children of thy creation, administer them comfort in time of trouble, and save them with an everlasting salvation. So mote it be. Amen.

The five-pointed star has been adopted, in very recent times, as a Masonic symbol. Differing, as it does, entirely from the blazing star, which in the first degree refers to Divine Providence, it is consecrated, in the third degree, as a symbol of the *Five Points of Fellowship.*

Among the Jews, as, indeed, among all other civilized nations, it was considered not only an act due to decency and humanity, but a religious obligation, to bury and pay honors to the dead. The bier was followed by mourners, who poured out the anguish of their hearts in lamentable wails, and who rehearsed the virtues of the departed, and expressed the sorrow of the survivors "Men," says JAHN, " who were distinguished for their rank, and who, at the same time, exhibited a claim to the love and favor of the people for their virtues and their good deeds, were honored with an attendance of vast multitudes, to witness the solemnities of their interment."

The Mosaic law which related to defilement by dead bodies, rendered it necessary that none should be buried near sacred places, nor even within the limits of cities, except in the case of kings and very distinguished men. The strictness of the religious code against pollution would, however, forbid that even these should be interred in the neighborhood of a temple or sanctuary.

As far back as the era of Abraham, sepulchral monuments are mentioned. When RACHEL died, we are told that JACOB "set a pillar upon her grave." The ancient Arabians erected a heap of stones over the dead; but as among the Hebrews such a heap was an indication that the body beneath had been stoned to death, the latter nation, therefore, confined their monuments to a single stone, which it was usual carefully to hew and to ornament with inscriptions.

Although among the early Jews the burning of the body was

esteemed disgraceful, the sentiment of the people was subsequently changed, and to burn the body with aromatic spices, and deposit *the ashes in an urn*, was considered, in the days of King Solomon, as a distinguished honor, while, says JAHN, "not to be burned was regarded a most signal disgrace."

We thus close the second section with a tribute to the memory of that distinguished artist who preferred to lose his life rather than betray his trust.

THIRD SECTION.

The third section furnishes many details in relation to the building of the Temple, and concludes with an explanation of the hieroglyphical emblems of the degree. Nearly all of this section is monitorial.

The Temple of King Solomon occupied seven years in its construction, during which time we are informed that it rained not in the daytime, that the workmen might not be obstructed in their labor.

This famous fabric was supported by fourteen hundred and fifty-three columns, and two thousand nine hundred and six pilasters, all hewn from the finest Parian marble.

It was symbolically supported, also, by three principal columns, *Wisdom*, *Strength*, and *Beauty*, which
were represented by the three Grand Masters, * * *

There were employed in its building three Grand
Masters; three thousand three hundred Overseers, or
masters of the work ; eighty thousand Fellow Crafts ;
and seventy thousand Entered Apprentices. All these
were classed and arranged by King Solomon, that
neither envy, discord, nor confusion were suffered to
interrupt that universal peace and tranquillity which
pervaded the world at this important period.

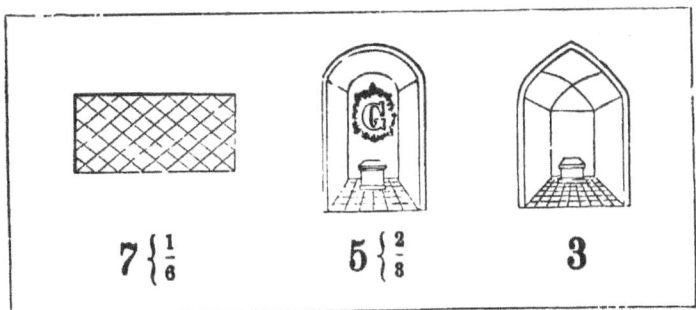

There are in this degree two classes of emblems or
symbols, the first of which is monitorial, and consists

of the *Three Steps*, the *Pot of Incense*, the *Bee-Hive*, the *Book of Constitutions, guarded by the Tiler's Sword*, the *Sword, pointing to a Naked Heart*, the *All-seeing Eye*, the *Anchor* and *Ark*, the *Forty-seventh Problem of Euclid*, the *Hour-Glass*, and the *Scythe*. They are thus explained :

THE THREE STEPS,

Usually delineated upon the Master's carpet, are emblematical of the three principal stages of human life, viz : *Youth, Manhood*, and *Age*. In *Youth*, as Entered Apprentices, we ought industriously to occupy our minds in the attainment of useful knowledge ; in *Manhood*, as Fellow Crafts, we should apply our knowledge to the discharge of our respective duties to God, our neighbor, and ourselves ; so that in *Age*, as Master Masons, we may enjoy the happy reflections consequent on a well-spent life, and die in the hope of a glorious immortality.

THE POT OF INCENSE

Is an emblem of a pure heart, which is always an acceptable sacrifice to the Deity; and as this glows with fervent heat, so should our hearts continually glow with gratitude to the great beneficent Author of our existence, for the manifold blessings and comforts we enjoy.

THE BEE-HIVE

Is an emblem of industry, and recommends the practice of that virtue to all created beings, from the highest seraph in heaven to the lowest reptile of the dust. It teaches us, that as we came into the world rational and intelligent beings, so we should ever be industrious ones; never sitting down contented while our fellow-creatures around us are in want, when it is in our power to relieve them without inconvenience to ourselves.

BOOK OF CONSTITUTIONS, GUARDED BY THE TILER'S SWORD, Reminds us that we should be ever watchful and guarded in our words and actions, particularly when before the enemies of Masonry; ever bearing in remembrance those truly Masonic virtues, *silence* and *circumspection*.

THE SWORD, POINTING TO A NAKED HEART,

Demonstrates that justice will sooner or later overtake us; and although our thoughts, words, and actions may be hidden from the eyes of men, yet that

ALL-SEEING EYE, whom the SUN, MOON, and STARS obey, and under whose watchful care even COMETS perform their stupendous revolutions, pervades the inmost recesses of the human HEART, and will reward us according to our merits.

THE ANCHOR AND ARK

Are emblems of a well-grounded *hope* and a well-spent life. They are emblem-atical of that divine *Ark* which safely wafts us over this tempest-uous sea of troubles, and that *Anchor* which shall safely moor us in a peaceful harbor, where the wicked cease from troubling, and the weary shall find rest.

THE FORTY-SEVENTH PROBLEM OF EUCLID.*

This was an invention of our ancient friend and brother, the great PYTHAGORAS, who, in his travels through Asia, Africa, and Europe, was initiated into several orders of priest-hood, and raised to the sublime degree of a Master Mason. This wise philosopher enriched

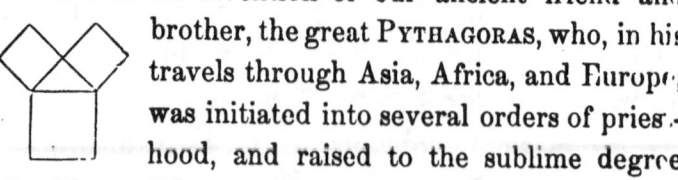

* This problem is thus enunciated by Euclid : "In any right-angled trian-gle, the square which is described upon the side subtending the right angle is equal to the square described upon the sides which contain the right angle.' —EUCLID, *Book I., Prob. 47.*

his mind abundantly in a general knowledge of things, and more especially in Geometry or Masonry. On this subject he drew out many problems and theorems; and among the most distinguished he erected this, when, in the joy of his heart, he exclaimed, *Eureka,* in the Grecian language signifying *I have found it;* and upon the discovery of which he is said to have sacrificed a hecatomb. It teaches Masons to be general lovers of the arts and sciences.

THE HOUR-GLASS

Is an emblem of human life. Behold! how swiftly the sands run, and how rapidly our lives are drawing to a close! We can not without astonishment behold the little particles which are contained in this machine; how they pass away almost imperceptibly! and yet, to our surprise, in the short space of an hour they are all exhausted. Thus wastes man! To-day he puts forth the tender leaves of hope; to-morrow blossoms, and bears his blushing honors thick upon him; the next day comes a frost, which nips the shoot; and when he thinks his greatness is still aspiring, he falls, like autumn leaves, to enrich our mother earth.

THE SCYTHE

Is an emblem of time, which cuts the brittle thread of life, and launches us into eternity. Behold! what havoc the scythe of Time makes among the human race! If by chance we should escape the numerous evils incident to childhood and youth, and with health and vigor arrive at the years of manhood; yet, withal, we must soon be cut down by the all-devouring scythe of Time, and be gathered into the land where our fathers have gone before us.

The second class of emblems are not monitorial, and therefore their true interpretation can only be obtained within the tiled recesses of the Lodge. They consist of the Setting Maul, the Spade, the Coffin, and the Sprig of Acacia. They afford subjects of serious and solemn reflection to the rational and contemplative mind, and thus the lecture closes with cheering promises of a blessed immortality beyond the grave.

CHARGE AT RAISING TO THE SUBLIME DEGREE OF A MASTER MASON.

BROTHER :

Your zeal for the institution of Masonry, the progress you have made in the mystery, and your conformity to our regulations, have pointed you out as a proper object of our favor and esteem. You are now bound by duty, honor, and gratitude to be faithful to your trust; to support the dignity of your character on every occasion; and to enforce, by precept and example, obedience to the tenets of the Order.

In the character of a Master Mason, you are authorized to correct the errors and irregularities of your uninformed brethren, and to guard them against a breach of fidelity. To preserve the reputation of the fraternity unsullied, must be your constant care; and for this purpose it is your province to recommend to your inferiors, obedience and submission; to your equals, courtesy and affability; to your superiors, kindness and condescension. Universal benevolence you are always to inculcate, and by the regularity of your own behavior afford the best example for the conduct of others less informed. The ancient landmarks of the Order, intrusted to your care, you are carefully to preserve; and never suffer them to be infringed, or countenance a deviation from the established usages and customs of the fraternity.

Your virtue, honor, and reputation are concerned in supporting with dignity the character you now bear. Let no motive, therefore, make you swerve from your duty, violate your vows, or betray your trust; but be true and faithful, and imitate the example of that celebrated artist whom you have this evening represented. Thus you will render yourself deserving of the honor which we have conferred, and merit the confidence that we have reposed.

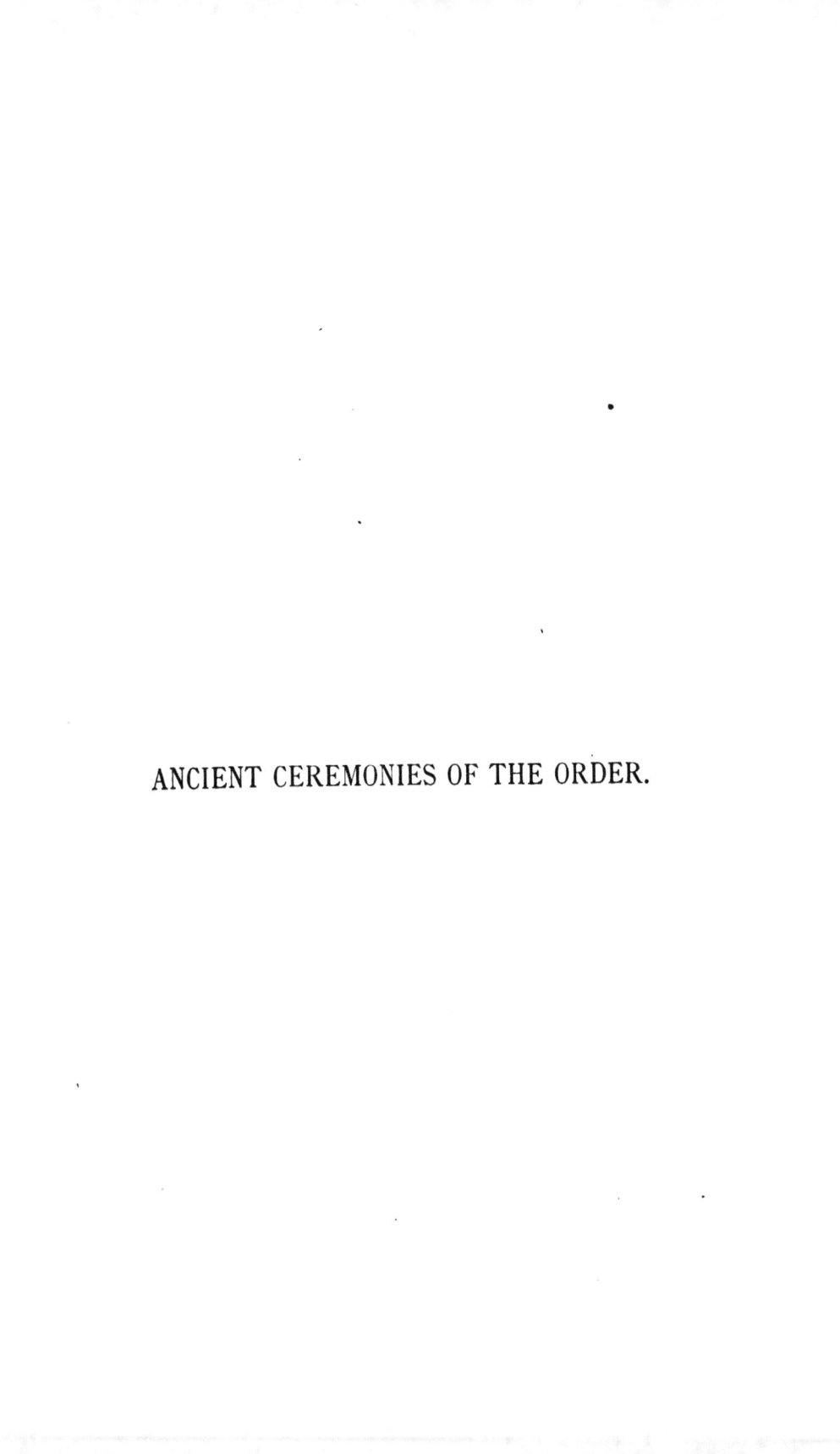

ANCIENT CEREMONIES OF THE ORDER.

ANCIENT CEREMONIES OF THE ORDER.

SECTION I.

CONSECRATION, DEDICATION, CONSTITUTION, AND INSTALLATION OF THE OFFICERS OF A NEW LODGE.

THOROUGH knowledge of these ceremonies is of the highest importance.
They should be well understood by
every Master of a Lodge. They treat
of the government of the society; the
disposition of its rulers, and illustrate
their proper functions and qualifications.

Any number of Master Masons, not
less than seven, having determined to
form a new Lodge, must apply by peti
tion to the Grand Master, which petition
should be in the following words:

*To the Most Worshipful Grand Master of Ancient
Freemasons of . . . .*

The petition of the undersigned respectfully showeth, that they are regular Freemasons, and are at

present or have been members of regular Lodges
that having the prosperity of the fraternity at heart,
they are willing to exert their best endeavors to promote and diffuse the genuine principles of Freemasonry ; that for the conveniency of their respective
dwellings [otherwise, stating the circumstances of the
case], and for other good reasons, they have agreed
to form a new Lodge ; that in consequence of this
resolution, they pray the Most Worshipful Grand
Master for a dispensation to empower them to
assemble as a regular Lodge at .... and there
to discharge the duties of Freemasonry in a regular
and constitutional manner, according to the ancient
usages of the Order, and the rules and regulations of
the Grand Lodge of Ancient Freemasons of . . . . .
. . . . ; that they have nominated and do recommend A. B. to be the first Master, and C. D. to be the
first Senior Warden, and E. F. the first Junior Warden
of the said Lodge : and the prayer of this petition
being granted, they promise strict conformity to every
regular edict and command of the Grand Master, and
to the constitutions, laws, and regulations of the Grand
Lodge of Ancient Freemasons of . . . .

This petition must be signed by, at least, seven regular Master Masons, and be recommended by the nearest Lodge, and be
delivered to the Grand Secretary, who shall present it to the
Grand Master, or, in his absence, to the Deputy Grand Master.
If the application shall be approved, the Grand Secretary is
ordered to grant a dispensation in the following words :

To all whom it may concern :

WHEREAS, we . . . . . . Most Worshipful Grand
Master of Ancient Freemasons of . . . . ,

have received a petition from a constitutional number of brethren who have been regularly vouched for and recommended, which petition sets forth that they are desirous of establishing a new Lodge at . . . under our Masonic jurisdiction, and requesting a dispensation for the same ; and whereas there appears to us good and sufficient cause for granting the prayer of the said petition—

Now know ye, that we, the Most Worshipful Grand Master aforesaid, by virtue of the powers in us vested by the Ancient Constitutions of the Order, do hereby grant this our dispensation, authorizing and empowering Brother . . . . . . to act as Worshipful Master, Brother . . . . . . to act as Senior Warden, and Brother . . . . . . to act as Junior Warden of a Lodge, to be held under our jurisdiction at . . . . and to be known as . . . . Lodge. And we further authorize and empower the said brethren to *Enter*, *Pass*, and *Raise* Freemasons according to the Ancient Constitutions of the Order, the customs and usages of the craft, and the rules and regulations of the Grand Lodge of Ancient Freemasons of . . . ., and not otherwise. And this our dispensation shall continue of force until the Grand Lodge shall grant a Warrant of Constitution for the same, or this dispensation be revoked by us or by the Grand Lodge aforesaid.

Given under our hand and the seal of the Grand [L. s.] Lodge, at the Grand East of . . . ., this . . . day of . . . . A∴ L∴ 58 . .

. . . .
Grand Secretary.   *Grand Master.*

A Lodge thus organized is said to be a Lodge under dispensation; and having been erected for a special purpose, is possessed of very limited powers. It is simply the creature of the Grand Master, and depends on his will for the duration of its existence. It can make no by-laws, but is governed by the general constitutions of the Order, and the rules and regulations of the Grand Lodge. It can not elect officers. The Master and Wardens are appointed by the Grand Master in the dispensation, and whatever other officers are necessary for carrying on the business of the Lodge must be appointed temporarily by the Master. As there can be no election, neither can there be any installation; for not even are the Master and Wardens of a Lodge under dispensation permitted to be thus solemnly inducted into office. A Lodge under dispensation can elect no members. The Master and Wardens who are named in the act of dispensation, are, in fact, the only persons recognized as constituting the Lodge. To them is granted the privilege, as proxies of the Grand Master, of making Masons; and for this purpose they are authorized to congregate a sufficient number of brethren to assist them in the ceremonies. But all persons who have been made Masons in a Lodge under dispensation, with all those engaged in holding it under the act of dispensation, become members as soon as it receives its Warrant of Constitution.

The act of dispensation continues of force, unless sooner revoked by the Grand Master, until the next regular communication of the Grand Lodge, before whom the petition, with the proceedings had thereon, must be laid. If the Grand Lodge approves of the same, it will grant a Warrant of Constitution, which is in the following form:

WARRANT OF CONSTITUTION.

To all whom it may concern:

The Most Worshipful Grand Lodge of Ancient Freemasons of . . . . in Grand Communication assembled, SEND GREETING:

Know ye, that we, the Grand Lodge of Ancient

Freemasons of . . . ., have authorized and empowered, and do hereby authorize and empower, our trusty and well-beloved brethren, A. B., Worshipful Master ; C. D., Senior Warden ; and E. F., Junior Warden, to open and hold a Lodge designated as . . . . . Lodge No. . ., under our register and jurisdiction at . . . ., in the State of . . . ., or within three miles of the same.

And we do further authorize and empower the said brethren to Admit, Enter, Pass, and Raise Freemasons, according to the most ancient customs and usages of the craft, in all ages and nations throughout the world, and not otherwise.

And we do further authorize and empower the said brethren, and their successors in office, to hear and determine all and singular, matters and things, relative to the craft, within the jurisdiction of the said Lodge.

.And lastly, we do hereby authorize, empower, and direct our said trusty and well-beloved brethren to install their successors in office, after being duly elected and chosen ; to invest them with all the powers and dignities to their offices respectively belonging, and to deliver to them this WARRANT OF CONSTITUTION ; and such successors shall, in like manner, from time to time, install their successors, and proceed in the premises as above directed : such installation to be upon, or immediately preceding, the festival of St. John the Evangelist, during the continuance of the said Lodge forever.

Provided always, that the said above-named brethren and their successors do pay, and cause to be paid, due respect and strict obedience to the Most Worshipful Grand Lodge of Ancient Freemasons of . . . . aforesaid, and to the rules, regulations, and edicts thereof; otherwise, this Warrant of Constitution to be of no force nor virtue.

> Given in open Grand Lodge, and under the hands of our Grand officers, and the seal of our Grand Lodge, at . . . ., this . . . day of . . . . ., in the year of Light, 58 . . .

Q . . . . R . . . .,   W . . . . V . . . .,
   Grand Master.   *Senior Grand Warden.*
S . . . . T . . . .,   [L. S.]   W . . . . X . . . .,
  Deputy Grand Master.   *Junior Grand Warden.*
     Y . . . . Z . . . ., *Grand Secretary.*

A new Lodge, for avoiding many irregularities, should be solemnly *consecrated, dedicated,* and *constituted,* and its officers *installed* by the Grand Master, with his Deputy and Wardens; or, in the Grand Master's absence, the Deputy shall act for him, the Senior Grand Warden as Deputy, the Junior Grand Warden as the Senior, and the Master of the oldest Lodge as the Junior; or, if the Deputy be also absent, the Grand Master may depute either of his Grand Wardens, who can appoint others to act as Grand Wardens *pro tempore.*

When a Warrant is granted for constituting a new Lodge at so great a distance as to render it inconvenient for the Grand officers to attend the ceremony, the Grand Master may issue a written instrument to some worthy brother, who has been regularly installed Master of a Lodge, empowering him to constitute the petitioners, and install their officers elect, when congregated by them, which instrument is in the following form :

To all whom it may concern :

But more especially to Brothers A. B., Worshipful Master elect; C. D., Senior Warden elect, and E. F.,

Junior Warden elect, and the rest of the brethren who have petitioned the Most Worshipful Grand Master for a Warrant of Constitution, to empower them to assemble as a regular Lodge, under the authority and Masonic jurisdiction of the Most Worshipful Grand Lodge of Ancient Freemasons of . . . .; the said petition having been granted and confirmed by the said Grand Lodge, at a . . . . communication held at . . . ., on the

Know ye, that reposing special trust and confidence in the Masonic talents, prudence, and integrity of our Worshipful Brother, ..., we have thought proper, ourselves being unable to attend, to constitute and appoint, and we do hereby constitute and appoint, our said Worshipful Brother . . . . . . our proxy, to constitute " IN FORM" the petitioners aforesaid into a Lodge, to be known and distinguished in our Register as . . . . Lodge No. . ., and to install their officers elect agreeably to ancient form and the custom of the craft; and for so doing, this shall be his sufficient warrant.

Given under our hand and seal of the Grand [L. S.] Lodge of Ancient Freemasons of . . . ., at . . . ., this . . . day of . . . . 58 .

. . . .
Grand Secretary.   *Grand Master.*

If the Grand and Deputy Grand Masters shall be absent, or rendered by sickness or casualty incapable of acting, the Grand Wardens may issue a like power under their hands and the Grand Seal, countersigned by the Grand Secretary; provided the Grand Master, or presiding officer, has previously signed a Warrant for holding such Lodge. But the Grand Wardens shall ʟ t issue any Masonic writing under their private seal or seals.

If t e Grand Master in person attend the ceremony, the Lodge is said to be constituted in AMPLE FORM; if the Deputy Grand Master only, it is said to be constituted in DUE FORM; but if the power of performing the ceremony be vested in any other person, it is said to be constituted in FORM.

CONSECRATION.

On the day and hour appointed, the Grand Master and his officers, or their representatives and proxies, meet in a convenient room near the Lodge to be consecrated, and open in the Third degree.

After the officers of the new Lodge are examined, they send a messenger to the Grand Master, with the following message:

MOST WORSHIPFUL: The officers and brethren of ...... Lodge, who are now assembled at ......, have instructed me to inform you, that the Most Worshipful Grand Lodge was pleased to grant them a charter, authorizing them to form and open a Lodge of Free and Accepted Masons in the town of ...... They are now desirous that their Lodge should be consecrated, and their officers installed in due and ancient form; for which purpose they are now met, and await the pleasure of the Most Worshipful Grand Master.

The Grand Lodge then walk in procession to the hall of the new Lodge. When the Grand Master enters, the grand honors are given by the new Lodge; the officers of which resign their seats to the Grand officers, and take their several stations on the left.

If the ceremonies are to be performed in public, the Grand Marshal then forms the procession in the following order:

Tiler, with drawn sword;
Two Stewards, with white rods;
Master Masons, two and two ;*
Junior Deacons, with rods;
Senior Deacons, with rods;
Secretaries, with rods;
Treasurers;
Junior Wardens, with columns;
Senior Wardens, with columns;
Masters of Lodges, with Hirams;
Past Masters;
Members of the higher Degrees

THE NEW LODGE.

Tiler, with a drawn sword.
Stewards, with white rods;
Master Masons;
Junior and Senior Deacons;
Secretary and Treasurer;
Two brethren carrying the Lodge;
Junior and Senior Wardens;
The Holy Writings, carried by the oldest or some
suitable member, not in office;
The Worshipful Master;
Music.

THE GRAND LODGE.

Grand Tiler, with drawn sword;
Junior Grand Deacons with rods;
Grand Pursuivant, with sword of state;
A brother carrying a Golden Vessel of Corn;
Two brethren, carrying the Silver Vessels, one of
Wine, the other of Oil;
Grand Secretary;
Grand Treasurer;
A burning Taper borne by a Past Master;
A Fast Master, bearing the Holy Writing, Square and Compasses,
supported by the Grand Stewards with white rods.
Two burning Tapers, borne by two Past Masters;
The Tuscan and Composite Orders;
The Doric, Ionic, and Corinthian Orders;
Past Grand Wardens;
Past Deputy Grand Masters;
Past Grand Masters;

* If there be any Entered Apprentices and Fellow Crafts, they may join
the procession outside of the Lodge, and will precede the Master Masons.

The Globes;
Grand Chaplain and Orator;
Junior and Senior Grand Wardens;
Deputy Grand Master;
The Master of the oldest Lodge, carrying the Book of Constitutions;
Grand Master,
supported by the Senior Grand Deacons.

The Marshals conduct the procession to the church or house where the services are to be performed. When the front of the procession arrives at the door, they halt, open to the right and left, and face inward, while the Grand Master and others, in succession, pass through and enter the house.

A platform is erected in front of the pulpit, and provided with seats for the accommodation of the Grand officers.

The Holy Bible, Square and Compasses, and Book of Constitutions are placed upon a table in front of the Grand Master; the Lodge is then placed in the center, upon the platform, covered with white satin or linen, and encompassed by the three tapers, and the vessels of *corn, wine,* and *oil.*

The following services then take place:

Great Source of light and love, To Thee our songs we raise!

O! in thy tem-ple, Lord, a-bove, Hear and ac-cept our praise!

Shine on this festive day,	May this fraternal band,
Succeed its hoped design,	Now *Consecrated*—blest,
And may our Charity display	In union all distinguished stand,
A love resembling thine.	In purity be drest.

Prayer by the Grand Chaplain.
An oration by some competent brother.
A piece of music.

The Grand Marshal forms the officers and members of the new Lodge in front of the Grand Master. The Deputy Grand Master addresses the Grand Master as follows:

MOST WORSHIPFUL: A number of brethren, duly instructed in the mysteries of Masonry, having assembled together at stated periods, by virtue of a dispensation granted them for that purpose, do now desire to be *constituted* into a *regular Lodge*, agreeably to the ancient usages and customs of the fraternity.

The dispensation and records are presented to the Grand Master, who examines the records, and, if found correct, proclaims:

The records appear to be correct, and are approved. Upon due deliberation, the Grand Lodge have granted the brethren of this new Lodge a Warrant, establishing and confirming them in the rights and privileges of a *regular constituted Lodge ;* which the Grand Secretary will now read.

After the Warrant is read, the Grand Master then says:

We shall now proceed, according to ancient usage, to constitute these brethren into a regular Lodge.

Whereupon the several officers of the new Lodge deliver up their jewels and badges to their Master, who presents them, with his own, to the Deputy Grand Master, and he to the Grand Master.

The Deputy Grand Master presents the Master elect to the Grand Master, saying,

MOST WORSHIPFUL : I present you Brother . . . . . .,
whom the members of the Lodge now to be constituted have chosen for their Master.

The Grand Master asks the brethren if they remain satisfied
with their choice. [*They bow in token of assent.*]

The Master elect then presents, severally, his Wardens and
other officers, naming them and their respective offices. The
Grand Master asks the brethren if they remain satisfied with
each and all of them. [*They bow as before.*]

The officers and members of the new Lodge form in front of
the Grand Master; and the business of *Consecration* commences.

The Grand Master, attended by the Grand officers, form themselves in order around the Lodge—all kneeling.

A piece of solemn music is performed while the Lodge is uncovered.

After which the first clause of the consecration prayer is rehearsed by the Grand Chaplain, which is as follows :

Great Architect of the Universe ! Maker and Ruler
of all worlds ! deign, from thy celestial temple, from
realms of light and glory, to bless us in all the purposes of our present assembly ! We humbly invoke
thee to give us at this, and at all times, *wisdom* in all
our doings, *strength* of mind in all our difficulties, and
the *beauty* of harmony in all our communications !
Permit us, O thou author of light and life, great source
of love and happiness, to erect this Lodge, and now
solemnly to *consecrate* it to the honor of thy glory !
Glory be to God on high.

Response by the Brethren.—As it was in the beginning, is now, and ever shall be ; world without end.
Amen.

The Deputy Grand Master presents the golden vessel of corn, and the Senior and Junior Grand Wardens the silver vessels of wine and oil, to the Grand Master, who sprinkles the elements of consecration upon the Lodge.

The Grand Chaplain then continues:

Grant, O Lord our God, that those who are now about to be invested with the government of this Lodge, may be endued with wisdom to instruct their brethren in all their duties. May *brotherly love, relief,* and *truth* always prevail among the members of this Lodge; may this bond of union continue to strengthen the Lodges throughout the world!

Bless all our brethren, wherever dispersed; and grant speedy relief to all who are either oppressed or distressed.

We affectionately commend to thee all the members of thy whole family. May they increase in grace, in the knowledge of thee, and in the love of each other.

Finally: may we finish all our work here below with thy approbation; and then have our transition from this earthly abode to thy heavenly temple above, there to enjoy light, glory, and bliss, ineffable and eternal!

Glory be to God on high.

Response.—As it was in the beginning, is now, and ever shall be. So mote it be. Amen.

DEDICATION.

A piece of solemn music is performed while the Lodge is un covered.

The Grand Master then standing with his hands stretched forth over the Lodge, exclaims, in an audible voice:

To the memory of the Holy SAINTS JOHN, we dedicate this Lodge. May every brother revere their character and imitate their virtues.

Glory be to God on high.

Response.—As it was in the beginning, is now, and ever shall be ; world without end. So mote it be. Amen.

A piece of music is performed while the brethren of the new Lodge advance in procession, to salute the Grand Lodge, with their hands crossed upon their breasts, and bowing as they pass. They then take their places as they were.

CONSTITUTION.

The Grand Master then rises and constitutes the new Lodge in the following form, all the brethren standing at the same time.

In the name of the Most Worshipful Grand Lodge, I now constitute and form you, my beloved brethren, into a regular Lodge of Free and Accepted Masons. From henceforth I empower you to meet as a regular Lodge, constituted in conformity to the rites of our Order, and the charges of our ancient and honorable fraternity ; and may the Supreme Architect of the Universe prosper, direct, and counsel you in all your doings.

Response.—So mote it be. Amen.

The public grand honors are then given by the brethren.

INSTALLATION OF THE OFFICERS OF A NEW LODGE.

The Lodge having been thus Consecrated, Dedicated, and Constituted, it is next required that the officers be installed.

The Grand Master or presiding officer says to his Deputy:

Right Worshipful Deputy, have you carefully examined the Master nominated in the Warrant, and do you find him well skilled in the mystic art?

The Deputy replies:

Most Worshipful Grand Master, I have carefully examined and so find him.

The Grand Master says:

You will then present him at the pedestal for installation.

The Deputy taking the Master elect from among his fellows, presents him at the pedestal, saying:

Most Worshipful Grand Master, I present my worthy Brother, A. B., to be installed Worshipful Master of this new Lodge. I find him to be of good morals and of great skill, true and trusty ; and as he is a lover of the fraternity, wheresoever dispersed over the face of the earth, I doubt not that he will discharge his duty with fidelity and with honor.

The Master then faces his brethren, and the Grand Master says:

Brethren, you now behold before the pedestal, Brother A. B., who has been duly nominated Wor-

The new Master then faces the East, and the presiding officer addresses to him the following charge:

Brother, previous to your investiture, it is necessary that you should signify your assent to those ancient charges and regulations which point out the duty of the Master of a Lodge.

I. Do you promise to be a good man and true, and strictly to obey the moral law?

Ans. I do.

II. Do you promise to be a peaceable citizen, and cheerfully to conform to the laws of the country in which you reside?

Ans. I do.

III. Do you promise not to be concerned in plots and conspiracies against the government of the country in which you live; but patiently to submit to the decision of the law and the constituted authorities?

Ans. I do.

IV. Do you promise to pay a proper respect to the civil magistrates, to work diligently, live creditably, and act honorably by all men?

Ans. I do.

V. Do you promise to hold in veneration the original rulers and patrons of the Order of Freemasonry, and their regular successors, supreme and subordinate, according to their stations; and to submit to the awards and resolutions of your brethren in Lodge convened, in every case consistent with the constitutions of the Order?

Ans. I do.

according to their stations ; and to submit to the awards and resolutions of your brethren in Lodge convened, in every case consistent with the constitutions of the Order ?

Ans. I do.

VI. Do you promise, as much as in you lies, to avoid private piques and quarrels, and to guard against intemperance and excess ?

Ans. I do.

VII. Do you promise to be cautious in your behavior, courteous to your brethren, and faithful to your Lodge ?

Ans. I do.

VIII. Do you promise to respect genuine and true brethren, and to discountenance impostors and all dissenters from the Ancient Landmarks and Constitutions of Masonry ?

Ans. I do.

IX. Do you promise, according to the best of your abilities, to promote the general good of society, to cultivate the social virtues, and to propagate the knowledge of the mystic art, according to our statutes ?

Ans. I do.

X. Do you promise to pay homage to the Grand Master for the time being, and to his officers when duly installed ; and strictly to conform to every edict of the Grand Lodge or General Assembly of Masons that is not subversive of the principles and groundwork of Masonry ?

Ans. I do.

XII. Do you promise a regular attendance on the committees and communications of the Grand Lodge, on receiving proper notice; and to pay attention to all the duties of Masonry, on convenient occasions?

Ans. I do.

XIII. Do you admit that no new Lodge can be formed without permission of the Grand Lodge; and that no countenance ought to be given to any irregular Lodge, or to any person clandestinely initiated therein, as being contrary to the ancient charges of the Order?

Ans. I do.

XIV. Do you admit that no person can be regularly made a Freemason in, or admitted a member of, any regular Lodge, without previous notice, and due inquiry into his character?

Ans. I do.

XV. Do you agree that no visitors shall be received into your Lodge without due examination, and producing proper vouchers of their having been initiated in a regular Lodge?

Ans. I do.

These are the regulations of Free and Accepted Masons.

The presiding officer then addresses the new Master as follows:

Do you submit to these charges, and promise to support these regulations, as Masters have done in all ages before you?

The Master is to answer, *I do.*

support these regulations, as Masters have done in all ages before you?

The Master is to answer, *I do.*

The presiding officer then addresses him:

Brother A. B., in consequence of your cheerful conformity to the charges and regulations of the Order, you are now to be installed Master of this new Lodge, in full confidence of your care, skill, and capacity to govern the same.

The new Master is then regularly invested with the insignia of his office, and the furniture and implements of his Lodge, accompanied by the following charge:

 The *Holy Writings*, that Great Light in Masonry, will guide you to all truth: it will direct your path to the temple of happiness, and point out to you the whole duty of man.

The *Square* teaches us to regulate our actions by rule and line, and harmonize our conduct by the principles of morality and virtue.

The *Compasses* teach us to limit our desires in every station; that rising to eminence by merit, we may live respected and die regretted.

The *Rule* directs that we should punctually observe 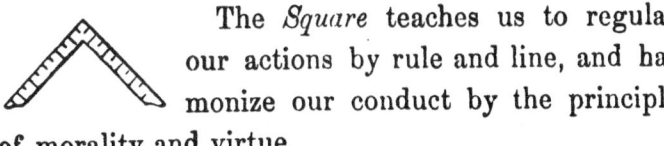 our duty; press forward in the path of virtue, and neither inclining to the right

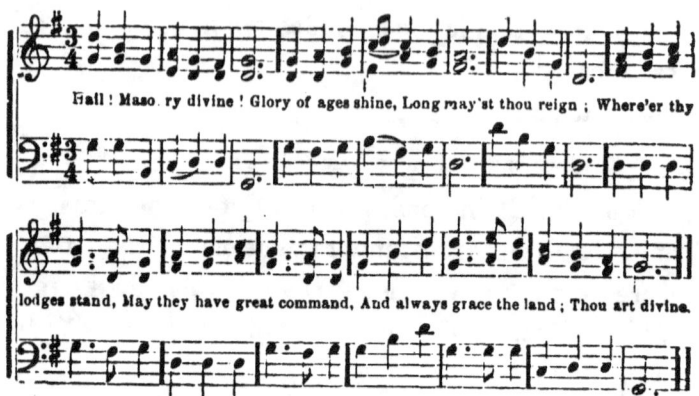

Hail! Maso.ry divine! Glory of ages shine, Long may'st thou reign ; Where'er thy

lodges stand, May they have great command, And always grace the land ; Thou art divine.

Hail, Masonry divine,
Glory of ages shine ;
   Long may'st thou reign !
Where'er thy Lodges stand,
May they have great command,
And always grace the land ;
   Thou art divine.

Great fabrics still arise,
And grace the azure skies—
   Great are thy schemes ;
Thy noble orders are
Matchless beyond compare ;
No art with thee can share ;
   Thou art divine.

Hiram, the architect,
Did all the craft direct
   How they should build ;
Sol'mon, great Israel's king,
Did mighty blessings bring.
And left us room to sing,
   Hail, Royal Art !

After the singing of the ode, the new Master calls the Lodge to order, and the Senior Warden is brought before him with the same ceremony as was used in his own case. No objection being made to his installation, the new Master administers the following obligation of office:

I, A. B., do solemnly promise that I will serve this Lodge as . . . . . . for the space of one year, from the festival of St. John the Evangelist to the one next ensuing, and will perform all the duties appertaining to that office, to the best of my abilities. So help me God.

The following charge is then rehearsed to him:

THE SENIOR WARDEN.

Brother C. D., you are appointed Senior Warden of this Lodge, and are now invested with the badge of your office.

The *Level* demonstrates that we are descended from the same stock, partake of the same nature, and share the same hope; and though distinctions among men are necessary to preserve subordination, yet no eminence of station should make us forget that we are brethren; for he who is placed on the lowest spoke of fortune's wheel, may be entitled to our regard; because a time will come, and the wisest knows not how soon, when all distinction, but that of good-ness, shall cease; and death, the grand leveler of human greatness, reduce us to the same state.

Your regular attendance on our stated meetings is essentially necessary. In the absence of the Master, you are to govern this Lodge; in his presence, you are to assist him in the government of it. I firmly rely on your knowledge of Masonry, and attachment to the Lodge, for the faithful discharge of the duties of this important trust.—*Look well to the West.*

The Senior Warden takes his appointed station.

The Junior Warden is then brought up with the same ceremonies; and the same obligation being administered, he receives the following charge:

THE JUNIOR WARDEN.

Brother E. F., you are appointed Junior Warden of this Lodge, and are now invested with the badge of your office.

The *Plumb* admonishes us to walk uprightly in our several stations; to hold the scales of justice in equal poise; to observe the just medium between intemperance and pleasure; and to make our passions and prejudices coincide with the line of our duty.

To you is committed the superintendence of the craft during the hours of refreshment; it is, therefore, indispensably necessary that you should not only be temperate and discreet in the indulgence of your own inclinations, but carefully observe that none of the craft be suffered to convert the purposes of refreshment into intemperance and excess

Your regular and punctual attendance is particularly requested; and I have no doubt that you will faithfully execute the duty which you owe to your present appointment.—*Look well to the South.*

The Junior Warden takes his appointed station.

Proclamation is then made as follows by the first presiding officer:

I hereby proclaim, that Brother A. B. has been duly installed as Worshipful Master, Brother C. D. as Senior Warden, and Brother E. F. as Junior Warden of . . . . . . Lodge, No. . ., with the grand honors of Masonry by three times three.

The grand honors are then given, and the new Master proceeds to install in like manner the rest of the officers, rehearsing to each his appropriate charge, as follows:

THE TREASURER.

Brother G. H., you are appointed Treasurer of this Lodge, and are now invested with the badge of your office. It is your duty to receive all moneys from the hands of the Secretary, make due entries of the same, and pay them out by order of the Worshipful Master and the consent of the Lodge.

I trust your regard for the fraternity will prompt you to the faithful discharge of the duties of your office.

THE SECRETARY.

Brother J. K., you are appointed Secretary of this Lodge, and are now invested with the badge of your office. It is your duty to observe all the proceedings of the Lodge; make a fair record of all things proper to be written; receive all moneys due the Lodge, pay them over to the Treasurer, and take his receipt for the same.

Your good inclination to Masonry and this Lodge, I hope, will induce you to discharge your office with fidelity ; and by so doing, you will merit the esteem and applause of your brethren.

SENIOR AND JUNIOR DEACONS.

Brothers L. M. and N. O., you are appointed Deacons 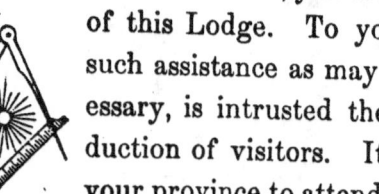 of this Lodge. To you, with such assistance as may be necessary, is intrusted the introduction of visitors. It is also your province to attend on the Master and Wardens, and to act as their proxies in the active duties of the Lodge ; such as in the reception of candidates into the different degrees of Masonry, and in the immediate practice of our rites. The *Square* and *Compasses*, as badges of your office, I intrust to your care, not doubting your vigilance and attention.

THE STEWARDS.

Brothers P. Q. and R. S., you are appointed Stewards of this Lodge, and are now invested with the badge of your office. The duties of your office are, to assist in the collection of dues and subscriptions ; to keep an account of the Lodge expenses ; to see that the tables are properly furnished at refreshment, and that every brother is suitably provided for ; and generally to assist the Deacons and other officers in performing their duties.

Your regular and early attendance will afford the best proof of your zeal and attachment to the Lodge.

THE TILER.

Brother T. U., you are appointed Tiler of this Lodge; and I invest you with the implement of your office. As the *Sword* is placed in the hands of the Tiler to enable him effectually to guard against the approach of cowans and eavesdroppers, and suffer none to pass or repass but such as are duly qualified; so it should morally serve as a constant admonition to us, to set a guard at the entrance of our thoughts; to place a watch at the door of our lips; to post a sentinel at the avenue of our actions, thereby excluding every unqualified and un-worthy thought, word, and deed; and preserving consciences void of offense toward God and toward man.

Your early and punctual attendance will afford the best proof of your zeal for the institution.

The officers having been thus installed, the new Master re-turns thanks, and the new officers resign their stations and places to the old officers, not to resume them again until St. John the Evangelist's day, when the Masonic year commences, unless the installation should have taken place on that day.

The Lodge is then closed.

SECTION III.

INSTALLATION OF THE OFFICERS OF A GRAND LODGE.

HE chair being taken by the Grand Master of the preceding year, or, in his absence, by some other Past Grand or Past Deputy Grand Master, the Grand Lodge is opened in the first degree of Masonry, so that all the craft may be permitted to be present. The other chairs are filled by the officers who, having served their time, are about to retire from office.

The Grand Secretary then reads from the records of the Grand Lodge the names of the officers who have been elected to serve for the ensuing year. The Grand Master elect, preceded by the Grand Marshal, is then conducted by two Senior Deacons to the front of the pedestal, and the Grand Marshal says to the presiding Grand officer:

Most Worshipful Sir, you here see present at the pedestal, Brother A. B., who, having been duly elected to preside over the craft as their Grand Master, now declares himself ready for installation.

The presiding Grand officer then rises and says:

Brethren, you here behold before the pedestal, Brother A. B., who, having been duly elected to preside over the craft as their Grand Master, now declares himself ready for installation. If any of you know of any reason why he should not be installed, you will state your objections now, or else forever hereafter hold your peace.

No objection being made, the presiding Grand officer proceeds to administer to the newly elected officer the obligation for the faithful discharge of his duties, the brethren all respectfully standing. The new Grand Master then receives the following charge, and being invested with the ensigns of his dignity, is placed in the Oriental Chair.

CHARGE TO THE GRAND MASTER.

Let me congratulate you, Most Worshipful Sir, on the honor of being raised, from the level of equality, to the high station of presiding over all the Lodges in the State of . . . ., and the Masonic jurisdiction thereof. We look up with confidence to a brother [whose age alone would entitle him to our respectful deference, but]* whose person is endeared to us by that love of the fraternity which is sanctified by the experience of many revolving years. May the Father of light, of life, and of love invest you with his choicest gifts ; may heavenly wisdom illumine your mind ; may heavenly power give strength to your exertions ; may heavenly goodness fill and enlarge your breast ; may your feet rest upon the rock of justice ; from your hands may streams of beneficence continually flow ; and round your head may there bend a circle made splendid by the rays of honor ; and late, very late in life, may you be transmitted from the fading honors of an earthly Lodge, to the mansions prepared for the faithful in another and a better world.

Let me congratulate you, the Grand officers, and other brethren, on the election of our [venerable]

* What is included within brackets, must be omitted as occasion may require.

Grand Master. As it is *his* duty to *command*, according to our constitutions, so it is *ours* with readiness to *obey*. Look to the sun, and behold the planetary worlds revolving round him in continual order and harmony with the happiest effect, and learn to imitate their regularity, in the hope of obtaining from the chair of *Solomon* the light of wisdom and the warmth of love. Or look higher still, and behold the cherubim and seraphim, who are exhibited to us in the oracles of revelation, as flaming spirits, burning with zeal and love before the throne of God. Behold the heavenly host, filled with love to their Creator, and love to our race. See these ministering spirits, exercising their kind offices to men, relieving their wants, securing them from danger, and endeavoring to promote their good.

> " Myriads of spiritual beings walk the earth
> Unseen, or when we sleep, or when we wake."

Of them let us learn, to rise in our affection to the great Father of all, and thence descending, expand the heart from brother to brother, and to all mankind. Of them let us learn, never to be weary in well-doing, but to "mourn with them that mourn, and to rejoice with them that do rejoice," until, having finished our work on earth, we shall be admitted to the temple above, "not made with hands, eternal in the heavens."

The Grand Marshal then standing in front of the pedestal says

Brethren, behold your Grand Master!

Grand Master, behold your brethren !

A procession of the craft is then made three times round the Lodge, and the INSTALLATION ODE is sung:

Hail ! Ma-son - ry di - vine ! Glo-ry of a - ges shine, Long may'st thou reign ; Where'er thy

lodges stand, May they have great command, And always grace the land : Thou art di-vine.

Hail, Masonry divine,
Glory of ages shine;
   Long may'st thou reign !
Where'er thy Lodges stand,
May they have great command,
And always grace the land;
   Thou art divine.

Great fabrics still arise,
And grace the azure skies—
   Great are thy schemes;
Thy noble orders are
Matchless beyond compare;
No art with thee can share;
   Thou art divine.

Hiram, the architect,
Did all the craft direct
   How they should build;
Sol'mon, great Israel's king,
Did mighty blessings bring,
And left us room to sing,
   Hail, Royal Art !

At the conclusion of the procession and ode, the Grand Mar shal makes the following proclamation:

By the authority of the Most Worshipful Grand Lodge of Ancient Freemasons of . . . ., I proclaim Most Worshipful Brother A. B. Grand Master of Masons, with the grand honors of Masonry by three times three.

The *public grand honors* are given by all the brethren.
The new Grand Master then proceeds to install the rest of the Grand officers, each of whom is introduced with the same ceremony before the pedestal, and presented by the Grand Marshal.

The Grand Marshal first introduces the Deputy Grand Master, saying:

Most Worshipful Sir, you here see present at the pedestal, Brother C. D., who having been duly elected to serve the craft as their Deputy Grand Master, now declares himself ready for installation.

The Grand Master says:

Brethren, you here behold before the pedestal, Brother C. D., who having been elected to serve the craft as their Deputy Grand Master, now declares himself ready for installation. If any of you know of any reason why he should not be installed, you will state your objections now, or else forever hereafter hold your peace.

No objection being made, the Grand Master proceeds to administer to the newly elected officer the obligation for the faithful discharge of his duties, the brethren all respectfully standing. The new Deputy Grand Master then receives the following charge, end being invested with the ensigns of his dignity, is placed at the right hand of the Grand Master:

DEPUTY GRAND MASTER.

Right Worshipful Brother, the station to which you have been called by the suffrages of your brethren, is one of great dignity and much importance. In the absence of the Grand Master, you are to exercise his prerogatives in presiding over the craft; in his presence you are to assist him with your counsel and co-operation. But while your powers and privileges are thus extensive, remember that they carry with them a heavy share of responsibility. The honor that has been conferred upon you, and the trust that has been reposed in you, demand a corresponding fidelity and attachment to the interests of those to whose kindness and confidence you are indebted for your official elevation. Let the Book of Constitutions be your constant study, that you may be the better enabled to preserve inviolate the laws and ancient landmarks of our Order, and that you may be ever ready to exercise the functions of that more exalted office to which you are so liable to be called. Receive this jewel of your office, and sit at our right hand to aid us with your counsel.

The remaining Grand officers are introduced in like manner, by the Grand Marshal, and receive their appropriate charges as follows :*

* When the former Grand Marshal has been re-elected, he is introduced to the pedestal by the Grand Pursuivant

SENIOR GRAND WARDEN.

Very Worshipful Brother, by the suffrages of your brethren, you have been elected their Senior Grand Warden, and we now invest you with the badge of your office.

Your regular attendance at the communications of the Grand Lodge is essentially necessary. In the absence of the Grand Master and his Deputy, you are to govern the craft; in their presence you are to strengthen and support the authority of your chief.

We firmly rely on your knowledge of Masonry and your attachment to our institution, for the faithful discharge of the duties of this important trust.—*Look well to the West.*

JUNIOR GRAND WARDEN.

Very Worshipful Brother, by the suffrages of your brethren, you have been elected their Junior Grand Warden, and we now invest you with the badge of your office.

Your regular and punctual attendance at the communications of the Grand Lodge is earnestly requested. In the absence of your superior officers, you are to govern the craft; in their presence you will aid them in their arduous labors.

We have no doubt that you will faithfully execute the duties which are incumbent on you in your present position.—*Look well to the South.*

GRAND TREASURER.

Worshipful Brother, you have been elected to the responsible office of Grand Treasurer, and we now invest you with the jewel of your office.

It is your duty to receive all moneys due the Grand Lodge, to make due entries of the same, and pay them out by order of the Grand Master, and with the consent and approbation of the Grand Lodge. The office to which you have been appointed embraces an important trust, and the choice of your brethren is an evidence of the high opinion they entertain of your fidelity and discretion.

We do not doubt that your regard for the fraternity will prompt you to the faithful discharge of your duties.

GRAND SECRETARY.

Worshipful Brother, you have been elected to the important office of Grand Secretary, and we now invest you with the jewel of your office.

It is your duty to observe all the proceedings of the Grand Lodge, and to make a fair record of all things proper to be written. You are also the official organ of the Grand Lodge, and in that capacity will conduct its various correspondence, and act as the medium of intercourse between the fraternity and their Grand Master. In the discharge of these extensive duties, let your carriage and behavior be marked by that promptitude and discretion that will at once reflect credit on yourself and honor on the body whom you represent

GRAND CHAPLAIN.

Most Reverend Brother, the sacred position of Grand Chaplain has been intrusted to your care, and we now invest you with the jewel of your office.

In the discharge of your duties you will be required to lead the devotional exercises of our Grand Communications, and to perform the sacred functions of your holy calling at our public ceremonies. Though Masonry be not religion, it is emphatically religion's handmaid, and we are sure that in ministering at its altar, the services you may perform will lose nothing of their vital influence because they are practiced in that spirit of universal tolerance which distinguishes our institution. The doctrines of morality and virtue, which you are accustomed to inculcate to the world, as the minister of God, will form the appropriate lessons you are expected to communicate to your brethren in the Lodge. The profession which you have chosen for your lot in life is the best guarantee that you will discharge the duties of your present appointment with steadfastness and perseverance in well-doing. The Holy Bible, that great light of Masonry, we intrust to your care.

GRAND LECTURER.

Worshipful Brother, you have been appointed the Grand Lecturer of this jurisdiction, and we now invest you with the jewel of your office.

It is your duty to instruct the craft in the due performance of their duty ; to communicate light and information to the uninformed ; to preserve our ritual and our traditions in the memory of the fraternity ; to see that the ancient landmarks of the Order are not removed by unskillful hands ; and by your instructions to the Subordinate Lodges, to illustrate the genius and vindicate the principles of our institution. It is to be presumed that one whom his brethren have thought capable of discharging so important and difficult a trust, will require no prompting for the proper performance of his duty. Let it be your object, while inculcating upon the members of this time-honored society a faithful regard for its obligations, to impress the world at large with a favorable opinion of its design and tendency.

GRAND DEACONS.

Brethren, you have been appointed the Grand Deacons of this Grand Lodge, and we now invest you with the jewels of your office, and these rods as ensigns of your authority.

It is your province to attend upon the Grand Mas

ter and Grand Wardens, and to act as their proxies in the active duties of the Grand Lodge. Let vigilance and attention actuate you in the discharge of the functions of your office.

GRAND MARSHAL.

Brother, you have been appointed Grand Marshal, and we now invest you with the jewel of your office, and present you with this baton, as the ensign of your authority.

It is your duty to proclaim the Grand officers at their installation; to arrange all processions of the Grand Lodge, and to preserve order according to the forms prescribed. Skill and precision are essentially necessary to the faithful discharge of these duties.

GRAND PURSUIVANT.

Brother, you have been appointed Grand Pursui vant, and we now invest you with the jewel of your office, and intrust thi sword of state to your keeping.

Your station is near the door, whence you will receive all reports from the Grand Tiler, and announce the name and Masonic rank of all who desire admission. You will see that none enter without wearing their appropriate decorations. You will also carry the Grand Sword of State in all public processions, and perform such other duties as appertain to your office. Your early and punctual attendance at all communications of the Grand Lodge is essentially necessary.

GRAND STEWARDS.

Brethren, you have been appointed Grand Stewards, and we now invest you with the jewels of your office, and place in your hands these white rods as ensigns of your station.

It is your duty to superintend the tables at the hour of refreshment, and see that every brother is suitably provided. It is, therefore, indispensably necessary that you yourselves should be temperate and discreet in the indulgence of your own inclinations, carefully observing that none of the craft transgress the due bounds of moderation in the enjoyment of their pleasures.

GRAND TILER.

Brother, you have been appointed Tiler of this Grand Lodge, and we now invest you with the jewel of your office, and place this sword in your hands, the more effectually to enable you to guard against the approach of cowans and eavesdroppers, and to suffer none to pass or repass but such as are duly qualified.

It is your duty to guard the door of the Grand Lodge on the outside; to report to the Grand Pursuivant those who desire to be admitted; to summon the members of the Grand Lodge, under the direction of the Grand Secretary, and to attend to such other duties as may be required of you by the Grand Lodge. Your punctual attendance is essentially necessary at every communication.

The Grand Marshal then makes proclamation as follows:

By the authority of the Most Worshipful Grand Lodge of Ancient Freemasons of ...., I proclaim that the Grand and Subordinate officers have been installed in ample form with the grand honors of Masonry by three times three.

The public grand honors are then given, and the brethren make the response,

So mote it be.

The following ODE, or some other appropriate one, is then sung:

Al-migh-ty Father! God of Love! Sacred, e-ternal King of kings

From thy celestial courts above, Send beams of grace on seraphs' wings.

Almighty Father! God of Love!
Sacred, eternal King of kings!
From thy celestial courts above,
Send beams of grace on seraphs' wings
Oh, may they, gilt with light divine,
Shed on our hearts inspiring rays:
While bending at this sacred shrine,
We offer mystic songs of praise.

Faith, with divine and heavenward eye,
   Pointing to radiant realms of bliss,
Shed here thy sweet benignity,
   And crown our works with happiness;
Hope! too, with bosom void of fear,
   Still on thy steadfast anchor lean;
Oh, shed thy balmy influence here,
   And fill our breasts with joy serene.

And thou, fair Charity! whose smile
   Can bid the heart forget its woe,
Whose hand can misery's care beguile,
   And kindness' sweetest boon bestow,
Here shed thy sweet soul-soothing ray;
   Soften our hearts, thou power divine!
Bid the warm gem of pity play,
   With sparkling luster, on our shrine.

Thou, who art thron'd 'midst dazzling light,
   And wrapp'd in brilliant robes of gold,
Whose flowing locks of silv'ry white
   Thy age and honor both unfold,
Genius of Masonry! descend,
   And guide our steps by thy strict law;
Oh, swiftly to our temple bend,
   And fill our breasts with solemn awe.

An address may then be delivered by any brother appointed for the occasion. After which the Grand Chaplain pronounces the benediction, and the Grand Lodge is closed in ample form.

SECTION IV.

CEREMONY OBSERVED AT GRAND VISITATIONS.

HE Grand Master, accompanied by the Grand officers, shall, at least once a year, or as often as he may deem expedient, visit the Lodges under his jurisdiction, to make the customary examinations. When this laudable duty becomes impracticable, from the extent of jurisdiction and large number of Lodges, the Grand Master may appoint any one or more of his Grand officers, who shall visit and inspect such Lodges as the Grand Master shall designate, and make report to him of the result.

The following is the form of a power for inspecting:

To all whom it may concern:

Know ye, that for divers good and sufficient reasons, we, the Most Worshipful Grand Master, finding it inconvenient in person to visit and inspect the following Lodges, namely [here insert the names and localities], have constituted and appointed, and by these presents do constitute and appoint, our Right Worshipful Brother, ... [here name his office], authorizing him as our special proxy to visit the aforesaid Lodges, and to inspect their proceedings, to ascertain the state of their funds and their general condition, report of the same to be forthwith made to me.

Given under our hand and the seal of the Grand
[L. S.]   Lodge, at . . . ., this . . . day of . . . ., in the year of Light, 58 . .

. . . ., ...,
Grand Secretary.   *Grand Master.*

When both the Grand and Deputy Grand Masters are absent, the Senior or Junior Grand Warden may preside, as Deputy, in visiting the Lodges, who, in such case, shall have the above deputation, under the grand seal, signed by the Grand Master, and countersigned by the Grand Secretary.

The following is the ceremony observed on such occasions:

The Grand Secretary, by command of the Grand Master or presiding Grand officer, notifies the Lodge of the intended visit.

The Master opens his Lodge in the third degree, and places his Deacons at the sides of the door, with their staves crossed. The brethren arrange themselves in a line from the door, on each side, to the chair. The orders, borne by some of the most respectable private brethren, wait near the door, to walk before the Grand officers when they enter. This being arranged in this manner, the Master deputes a Past Master to escort the Grand officers, who enter in the following form:

Grand Marshal;

Grand Stewards;

Grand Pursuivant, with sword of state;

Two Grand Deacons;

Grand Treasurer and Secretary;

Grand Chaplain;

Senior and Junior Grand Wardens;

Grand and Deputy Grand Masters;

Two Grand Deacons.

The Grand Tiler remains at the door.

They proceed up to the East, when they open to the right and left, and the Grand Master passes through to the chair; they then close, and take their seats on the right of the Master. The Master receives the Grand Master according to ancient usage, with the private grand honors of Masonry, and resigns to him the chair and the hiram, when the officers of the Lodge resign their seats to the corresponding Grand officers. The Master then delivers to the Grand Master the Warrant of Constitution, the Treasurer's and Secretary's books, and a statement of the funds of the Lodge, for his inspection. Having examined them, he

expresses his approbation, or makes such observations as the cir
cumstances and situation of the Lodge may require.   The Grand
Master then resigns the chair to the Worshipful Master, and the
Grand officers leave their seats, and repair to the East.

Should the Grand officers retire before the Lodge is closed, the
same ceremony must be observed as at their entrance.

———◆·◆———

SECTION V.

FESTIVALS OF THE ORDER.

N every country where Freemasonry is en
couraged, its festival days are celebrated
with great ceremony.   These are, the festival
of St. John the Baptist, on the 24th of June,
and that of St. John the Evangelist, on the 27th
of December.   They are days set apart by the
fraternity to worship the Grand Architect of
the Universe; to implore his blessings upon the
great family of mankind; and to partake of the
feast of brotherly affection.   Hence the Grand
Lodge has recommended to every Lodge, annually to celebrate one or both of these days in
such way as will be most conducive to the ad-
vantage of the Lodge, and the honor and benefit of the Institution.

Whichever day may have been selected, the Lodge about to
celebrate it should assemble at its usual place of meeting, and
having been opened on the first degree, is called from labor, and
a procession is to be formed as follows:

Tiler, with his sword;
Two Stewards, with white staves;
Two Standards (Faith and Hope);
Entered Apprentices, two and two;

Fellow Crafts, two and two;
Master Masons, two and two;
Two Standards (Charity and Wisdom);
Masons of the higher degrees;
A Brother, carrying one of the Orders;
Four Brethren carrying the other four Orders, two and two;
Two Standards (Strength and Beauty);
Secretary and Treasurer;
The oldest members of the Lodge carrying the Holy Bible,
Square, and Compasses;
Chaplain and Orator;
Past Wardens;
Past Masters;
The two Wardens, with their pillars;
Junior Deacon, Worshipful Master, Senior Deacon.

If any Grand officers be present, they must be placed in the rear of the procession, immediately in front of the two Wardens.

Every officer must wear the jewels of his office. The Marshal attends on horseback to regulate the procession. On arriving at the church gate, the brethren uncover and open their ranks to the right and left as far as the Master, who, followed by the brethren, passes between the lines, likewise uncovered, into the church. The same ceremony is observed on their return to the Freemasons' Hall.

Divine service must be performed by the Chaplain, and an appropriate address delivered by some competent brother appointed for the occasion. Hymns and anthems adapted to the occasion shall be sung, and after service, a collection may be made at the church doors, in aid of the charity fund. After the return to the hall, the Master may deliver a charge from the chair, upon such subjects connected with the Order, and the honor and happiness of the craft, as he may think proper.

In all Masonic processions, no Freemason shall wear the insignia of any Order which is not recognized by the Grand Lodge. The proper dress of Freemasons in procession is, black clothes, with white gloves and stockings.

When the day is celebrated by the Grand Lodge, the procession must be formed as follows:

Tiler, with his sword;
Two Deacons, with their staves;
Two Standards (Faith and Hope);
Twelve Fellow Crafts, two and two;
Tiler, with his sword;
Entered Apprentices, two and two;
Fellow Crafts, two and two;
Master Masons, two and two;
Tiler, with his sword;
Two Deacons, with their staves;
Two Deacons, with staves;
Two Standards (Strength and Beauty);
Music;
Grand Tiler, with flaming sword;
Grand Stewards, with white rods;
A Brother, carrying one of the Orders;
Four Brethren, carrying the other four Orders, two and two:
Grand Pursuivant, with sword of state;
Grand Secretary, with his bag;
Grand Treasurer, with his staff;
The Bible, Square, and Compasses, on a crimson velvet cushion, carried
by an aged Master Mason, supported by two Deacons, with their staves;
Grand Chaplain and Orator;
Past Grand Wardens;
Past Deputy Grand Masters;
Past Grand Masters;
Junior Grand Deacons, with their staves;
Grand Wardens, with their pillars;
Deputy Grand Master:
The Book of Constitutions, on a crimson velvet cushion, carried
by the Master of the oldest Lodge;
Grand Master;
Senior Grand Deacons, with their staves;
Two Tilers, with drawn swords, close the procession.

Grand Marshal.   *Assistant Marshal.*

These forms of procession may be used by the Grand or a Subordinate Lodge on all other public occasions where a particular form is not laid down in this work.

SECTION VI.

AT LAYING THE FOUNDATION STONES OF PUBLIO STRUCTURES.

HIS ceremony must only be performed by the Grand Master, assisted by the Grand Lodge, in General Communication. The chief magistrate, and other civil officers of the place where the building is to be erected, generally attend on the occasion. The ceremony is thus conducted:

At the time appointed, the brethren are convened at some convenient place, approved of by the Grand Master. A band of music is provided, and the brethren appear in the insignia of the Order, well dressed, with white gloves and aprons. The Grand Lodge is opened in the first degree, by the Grand Master, and the rules for regulating the procession to and from the place where the ceremony is to be performed, are read by the Grand Secretary. The necessary cautions are then given from the chair, and the Grand Lodge is called off from labor, after which, the procession, being arranged by the Grand Marshal, sets out in the following order:

Tiler, with drawn sword;
Two Deacons, with staves;
Two Standards (Faith and Hope);
Twelve Fellow Crafts, two and two;
Tiler, with drawn sword;
Entered Apprentices, two and two;
Fellow Crafts, two and two;
Master Masons, two and two;
Tiler, with drawn sword;
Two Deacons, with staves,
Two Standards (Charity and Wisdom):
Secretaries of Lodges, with rolls, two and two

Treasurers of Lodges, with green bags, two and two;

Junior Wardens of Lodges, with pillars, two and two·

Senior Wardens of Lodges, with pillars, two and two;

Masters of Lodges, with hirams, two and two:

Past Masters of Lodges, two and two;

Masons of such of the higher degrees as are recognized by the Grand
Lodge, in the form of their respective Orders;

Tiler, with drawn sword;

Two Deacons, with staves;

Two Standards (Strength and Beauty);

Grand Tiler, with drawn sword;

Grand Stewards, with white rods;

Music;

A brother, carrying one of the Orders;

Architect, with some implement of his office;

Four brethren, carrying the four Orders, two and two;

Grand Pursuivant, with sword of state;

Grand Secretary, with his bag;

Grand Treasurer, with his staff;

The Bible, Square, and Compasses, on a crimson velvet cushion, carried
by an aged Master Mason, supported by two Deacons with staves:

Grand Chaplain;

Past Grand Wardens;

Past Deputy Grand Masters;

Past Grand Masters;

Chief magistrate and civil officers of the place;

Two Junior Grand Deacons, with staves;

Grand Wardens;

Deputy Grand Master;

Book of Constitutions, carried by the Master of the oldest Lodge;

Grand Master, supported by two Senior Grand Deacons, with staves;

Two Tilers, with swords drawn, close the procession.

The Grand Marshal attends on horseback to regulate the procession.

A triumphal arch is erected at the place where the ceremony is to be performed.

The procession arriving at the arch, opens to the right and left, and, uncovering, the Grand Master and his officers repair to a temporary platform, covered with a carpet, and the rest of the brethren surround the platform. The Grand Master commands silence in the usual Masonic form, when the following Ode is sung:

When earth's founda - tion first was laid, By the Al - migh - ty

Ar-tist's hand, 'Twas then our perfect, our perfect, laws were made, Es

- tablished by his strict command.   Hail! mysterious, hail,

glorious Mason - ry! that makes us e - ver great and free.

When earth's foundation first was laid
  By the Almighty Artist's hand,
'Twas then our perfect, our perfect laws were made,
  Established by his strict command.

CHORUS.

  Hail, mysterious—hail, glorious Masonry,
  That makes us ever great and free.

In vain mankind for shelter sought,
  In vain from place to place did roam,
Until from heaven, from heaven they were taught
  To plan, to build, to fix their home.

    CHORUS.—Hail, etc.

Illustrious hence we date our Art,
  Which now in beauteous piles appear,
And shall to endless, to endless time impart,
  How worthy and how great we are.

    CHORUS.—Hail, etc.

Nor we less fam'd for every tie
  By which the human thought is bound;
Love, truth, and *friendship,* and friendship socially,
  Join all our hearts and hands around.

    CHORUS.—Hail, etc.

Our actions still by virtue blest,
  And to our precepts ever true,
The world admiring, admiring shall request
  To learn, and our bright paths pursue.

    CHORUS.—Hail, etc.

The necessary preparations are then made for laying the stone, on which is engraved the year of Masonry, the name of the Grand Master, and such other particulars as may be deemed necessary.

The stone is raised up by means of an engine, erected for that purpose in the northeast corner of the intended building.

The Grand Chaplain offers up a short prayer.

The Grand Treasurer then, by the Grand Master's command, places under the stone various sorts of coin and medals of the present age. Solemn music is introduced, and the stone is let down into its place by three gradual motions.

The principal architect then presents the working tools to the Grand Master, who, descending to the foundation, applies the *plumb*, *square*, and *level* to the stone, in their proper positions, and standing in front of all, says in a loud voice:

I have tried and proved this stone by plumb, square, and level, and pronounce it to be WELL-FORMED, TRUE, and TRUSTY.

The Deputy Grand Master then presents the Grand Master with the golden vessel of corn, saying:

Most Worshipful, I present you with the corn of nourishment.

The Grand Master then scatters the corn upon the stone, and the Senior Grand Warden presents him with the silver vessel of wine, saying:

Most Worshipful, I present you with the wine of

The Grand Master pours the wine upon the stone, and the Junior Grand Warden presents him with the silver vessel of oil, saying:

Most Worshipful, I present you with the oil of joy.

The Grand Master pours the oil upon the stone, and standing in front of all, and extending his hands, he makes the following invocation:

May the all-bounteous Author of Nature bless the inhabitants of this place with all the necessaries, conveniences, and comforts of life; assist in the erection and completion of this building; protect the workmen against every accident; long preserve this structure from decay; and grant to us all a supply of the CORN of *nourishment,* the WINE of *refreshment,* and the OIL of *joy.* So mote it be. Amen.

The Grand Master then strikes the stone *three times* with his hiram, and the brethren give the public grand honors of Masonry by three times three.

The Grand Master then ascends the platform, and delivers over the various implements of architecture to the architect, saying:

Worthy Sir (or Brother), having thus, as Grand Master of Masons, laid the foundation stone of this structure, I now deliver these implements of your profession into your hands, intrusting you with the superintendence and direction of the work, having full confidence in your skill and capacity to conduct the same.

The Grand Master then reascends the platform, and the following ANTHEM is sung:

1. Let there be light! th' Almighty spoke; Refulgent streams from
cha - os broke, T'illume the ris - ing earth! Well
pleas'd the great Je-ho - vah stood, The Pow'r su-preme pronounc'd it good, And gave the plan - ets birth! In

cho-ral numbers let us join To bless and praise this light divine!

"Let there be light!" th' Almighty spoke:
Refulgent streams from chaos broke,
   To illume the rising earth!
Well pleas'd the great JEHOVAH stood;
The power Supreme pronounc'd it good,
   And gave the planets birth!

CHORUS.—In choral numbers Masons join,
     To bless and praise this light divine.

Parent of light, accept our praise!
Who shedd'st on us thy brightest rays,
   The light that fills the mind:
By choice selected, lo! we stand,
By friendship join'd a social band!
   That love, that aid mankind!

    CHORUS.—In choral numbers, etc.

The widow's tear, the orphan's cry,
All wants our ready hands supply,
   As far as power is given;
The naked clothe, the pris'ner free,
These are thy works, sweet Charity,
   Reveal'd to us from heaven.

    CHORUS.—In choral numbers, etc.

The Grand Master then addresses the assembly as follows:

Men and brethren here assembled, be it known unto you, that we be lawful Masons, true and faithful to the laws of our country, and engaged, by solemn obligations, to erect magnificent buildings, to be serviceable to the brethren, and to fear God, the Great Architect of the Universe. We have among us, concealed from the eyes of all men, secrets which can not be divulged, and which have never been found out; but these secrets are lawful and honorable, and not repugnant to the laws of God or man. They were intrusted, in peace and honor, to the Masons of ancient times, and having been faithfully transmitted to us, it is our duty to convey them unimpaired to the latest posterity. Unless our craft were good and our calling honorable, we should not have lasted for so many centuries, nor should we have been honored with the patronage of so many illustrious men in all ages, who have ever shown themselves ready to promote our interests and defend us from all adversaries. We are assembled here to-day in the face of you all, to build a house, which we pray God may deserve to prosper, by becoming a place of concourse for good men, and promoting harmony and brotherly love throughout the world, till time shall be no more.

The brethren all exclaim:

So mote it be. Amen.

A voluntary collection is then made by the Grand Stewards among the brethren for the needy workmen, and the sum collected is placed upon the stone by the Grand Treasurer; during which time the following Song is sung in honor of Masonry:

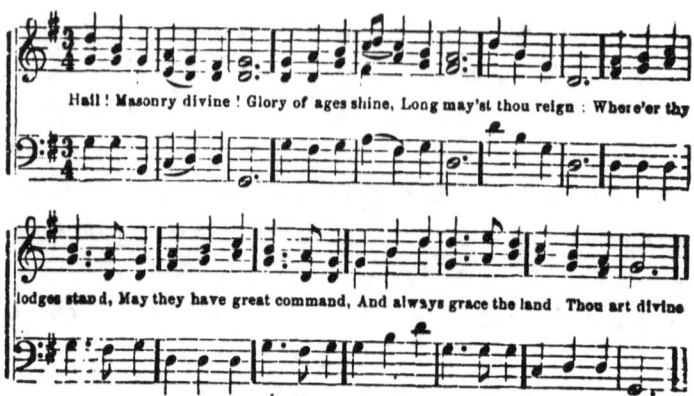

Hail! Masonry divine! Glory of ages shine, Long may'st thou reign : Where'er thy

lodges stand, May they have great command, And always grace the land. Thou art divine

Hail, Masonry divine,
Glory of ages shine ;
   Long may'st thou reign !
Where'er thy Lodges stand,
May they have great command
And always grace the land .
   Thou art divine.

Great fabrics still arise,
And grace the azure skies—
   Great are thy schemes ;
Thy noble orders are
Matchless beyond compare ;
No art with thee can share :
   Thou art divine.

Hiram, the architect,
Did all the craft direct
   How they should build ;
Sol'mon, great Israel's king
Did mighty blessings bring,
And left us room to sing.
   Hail, Royal Art !

A benediction is then pronounced by the Grand Chaplain after which the procession returns in the same order to the place whence it set out, and the Grand Lodge is closed with the usual formalities.

Where the site of the intended building is too remote for the Grand Master to attend in person, a dispensation may be obtained by the nearest Subordinate Lodge to perform the ceremony as near to the customary forms as circumstances will permit.

SECTION VII.

DEDICATION OF FREEMASONS' HALLS.

N the day appointed for the celebration of the ceremony of dedication, the brethren are convened in a convenient room, adjoining to the place where the ceremony is to be performed, and the Grand Lodge is opened in ample form in the first degree. The order of procession is read by the Grand Secretary, and a general charge respecting propriety of behavior given by the Grand Master. The Grand Lodge then moves to the Hall which is to be dedicated, in the following form of procession:

Tiler, with drawn sword;
Two Deacons, with rods;
Two Standards (Faith and Hope);

Twelve Fellow Crafts, two and two;
Tiler, with drawn sword;
Entered Apprentices, two and two;
Fellow Crafts, two and two;
Master Masons, two and two;
Tiler, with drawn sword;
Two Deacons, with rods;
Two Standards (Charity and Wisdom);
Secretaries of Lodges, with rolls, two and two;
Treasurers of Lodges, with their badges of office, two and two
Junior Wardens of Lodges, with pillars, two and two;
Senior Wardens of Lodges, with pillars, two and two;
Masters of Lodges, with hirams, two and two;
Past Masters of Lodges, two and two;
Masons of such of the higher degrees as are recognized by the Grand
Lodge, in the form of their respective Orders;
Tiler, with drawn sword;
Two Deacons, with rods;
Two Standards (Strength and Beauty);
Grand Tiler, with drawn sword;
Grand Stewards, with white staves;

Music;

A Brother, carrying a gold pitcher, containing corn;
Two Brethren, with silver pitchers, containing oil and wine;
A Brother, carrying one of the Orders:
Four Brethren, carrying the LODGE, covered with white silk;
Four Brethren, carrying the other four Orders, two and two;
Architect, with square, level, and plumb;
Grand Pursuivant, with sword of state;
Grand Secretary, with a green bag;
Grand Treasurer, with his staff;
Bible, Square, and Compasses, on a crimson velvet cushion, carried by
an aged Mason, supported by two Deacons, with their rods;
Grand Chaplain and Orator;
Past Grand Wardens;
Past Deputy Grand Masters;
Past Grand Masters;
Chief Magistrate and civil Officers of the place;
Junior Grand Deacons, with rods;
Grand Wardens;
Deputy Grand Master;
The Constitutions, carried on a crimson velvet cushion, by the
Master of the oldest Lodge;
Grand Master;
Senior Grand Deacons, with rods;
Two Tilers, with swords drawn, close the procession.

Marshal.

Grand Marshal.

Every officer must wear the jewel of his office. The Grand Marshal attends on horseback to regulate the procession and preserve order. In all Masonic processions, the brethren open to the right and left, as far as the Grand Tiler, and the Grand officers and regalia pass through—the brethren being uncovered.

When the procession reaches the Grand Master's chair, the Grand officers are separately proclaimed by the Grand Marshal, according to rank, as they arrive at that station, and when the Grand Master is proclaimed, a grand piece of music is performed, while the procession is made *three* times round the Hall. The Lodge is then placed in the center, and the Grand Master having taken the chair, under a canopy of state, the Grand officers and the Masters and Wardens of the Lodges, etc., repair to the places previously prepared for their reception. The five Orders are arranged near the Lodge, and the gold and silver pitchers, with the corn, wine, and oil, are placed upon it. Near it stands a pedestal, with the Bible open, and the square and compasses laid thereon, and upon another pedestal, the Book of Constitutions. These arrangements being made, the following ANTHEM, or some other appropriate one, is sung:

Hail, universal Lord,
By heaven and earth adore.
  All hail, great God!
Before thy throne we bend,
To us thy grace extend,
And to our prayer attend;
  All hail, great God!

O, hear our prayer to-day,
Turn not thy face away,
  O Lord our God!
Heaven, thy dread dwelling-place
Can not contain thy grace;
Remember now our race,
  O Lord our God!

God of our fathers, hear,
And to our cry be near,
  Jehovah, God!
The heavens eternal bow,
Forgive in mercy now
Thy suppliants here, O thou
  Jehovah, God!

To thee our hearts do draw,
On them, O write thy law,
  Our Saviour God!
When in this Lodge we're met,
And at thine altar set,
O, do not us forget,
  Our Saviour God!

The Master of the Lodge to which the Hall to be dedicated belongs, then rises, and approaching the East addresses the Grand Master as follows:

The brethren of ...... Lodge, being animated with a desire to promote the honor and interest of the craft, have erected a Masonic Hall for their convenience and accommodation. They are desirous that the same should be examined by the Most Worshipful Grand Lodge, and if it should meet their approbation, that it should be solemnly dedicated to Masonic purposes agreeably to ancient form and usage.

The Architect then addresses the Grand Master as follows, presenting to him the Square, Level, and Plumb:

Most Worshipful, having been intrusted with the superintendence and management of the workmen employed in the construction of this edifice, and having, according to the best of my ability, accomplished the task assigned me, I now return my thanks for the honor of this appointment, and beg leave to surrender up the implements which were committed to my care, when the foundation of this fabric was laid; humbly hoping, that the exertions which have been made on this occasion, will be crowned with your approbation, and that of the Most Worshipful Grand Lodge.

To which the Grand Master makes the following reply:

Brother Architect, the skill and fidelity displayed in the execution of the trust reposed in you, at the commencement of this undertaking, have secured the entire approbation of the Grand Lodge; and they sincerely pray that this edifice may continue a lasting monument of the taste, spirit, and liberality of its founders.

The Deputy Grand Master then rises, and says:

Most Worshipful, the hall in which we are now assembled, and the plan upon which it has been constructed, having met with your approbation, it is the desire of the fraternity that it should now be dedicated, according to ancient form and usage.

The Lodge is then uncovered, and a procession is made around it in the following form, during which solemn music is played:

Grand Pursuivant;
Two Stewards, with staves;
A Past Master, with a light;
A Past Master, with Bible, Square, and Compasses on a velvet cushion;
Two Past Masters, each with a light;
Grand Secretary and Treasurer;
Grand Junior Warden, with pitcher of corn;
Grand Senior Warden, with pitcher of wine;
Deputy Grand Master, with pitcher of oil;
Grand Master;
Two Deacons, with rods.

When the Grand Master arrives at the East, the procession halts, the music is silent, and the Grand Chaplain makes the following

CONSECRATION PRAYER.

Almighty and ever glorious and gracious Lord God, Creator of all things, and Governor of everything thou hast made, mercifully look upon thy servants, now assembled in thy name and in thy presence, and bless and prosper all our works begun, continued, and ended in thee. Graciously bestow upon us *Wisdom*, in all our doings; *Strength* of mind in all our difficul-

ties, and the *Beauty* of harmony and holiness in all
our communications and work. Let *Faith* be the
foundation of our *Hope*, and *Charity* the fruit of our
obedience to thy revealed will.

O thou preserver of men! graciously enable us now
to dedicate this house which we have erected, to the
honor and glory of thy name, and mercifully be pleased
to accept this service at our hands.

May all who shall be lawfully appointed to rule
herein according to our Constitutions, be under thy
special guidance and protection, and faithfully observe
and fulfill all their obligations to thee and to the Lodge.

May all who come within these consecrated walls,
have but one heart and one mind, to love, to honor,
to fear, and to obey thee, as thy majesty and un-
bounded goodness claim ; and to love one another, as
thou hast loved us. May every discordant passion be
here banished from our bosom. May we here meet
in thy presence as a band of brethren, who were
created by the same Almighty Parent, are daily sustained by the same beneficent hand, and are traveling
the same road to the gates of death. May we here
have thy Holy Word always present to our mind, and
religion, and virtue, love, harmony, and peaceful joy
reigning triumphant in our hearts.

May all the proper work of our institution that
may be done in this house be such as thy wisdom
may approve and thy goodness prosper. And finally,
graciously be pleased, O thou Sovereign Architect of
the Universe, to bless the craft wheresoever dispersed,
and make them true and faithful to thee, to their

neighbor, and to themselves. And when the time of our labor is drawing near to an end, and the pillar of our strength is declining to the ground, graciously enable us to pass through the valley of the shadow of death, supported by thy rod and thy staff, to those mansions beyond the skies where love, and peace, and joy forever reign before thy throne.—Amen.

Response by the Brethren.—Glory be to God on high, on earth peace, good-will toward men.

The Junior Grand Warden then presents the vessel of *corn to* the Grand Master, who pours it upon the LODGE, saying :

In the name of the Supreme and Eternal God, the Grand Architect of heaven and earth, to whom be all honor and glory, I dedicate this hall to FREEMASONRY.

The public grand honors are then given.

A piece of music is then performed, and the second procession is made round the Lodge. When the Grand Master arrives at the East, the music ceases, and the Senior Grand Warden presents him with the vessel of *wine*, which he sprinkles over the LODGE, saying :

In the name of the Supreme and Eternal God, the Grand Architect of heaven and earth, to whom be all honor and glory, I dedicate this hall to VIRTUE.

The public grand honors are then given.

The music is resumed, and the third procession is made round the Lodge. When the Grand Master arrives at the East, the music ceases, and the Deputy Grand Master presents him with the vessel of *oil*, which he sprinkles over the LODGE, saying:

In the name of the Supreme and Eternal God, the Grand Architect of heaven and earth, to whom be all honor and glory, I dedicate this hall to UNIVERSAL BENEVOLENCE.

The public grand honors are then given.

The Grand Chaplain, standing before the LODGE, then makes the following

INVOCATION.

O Lord God, there is no God like unto thee, in heaven above, or in the earth beneath, who keepest covenant and mercy with thy servants, who walk before thee with all their hearts.

Let all the people of the earth know that the Lord is God; and that there is none else. Let all the people of the earth *know* thy *Name*, and fear thee.

Let all the people know that this house is built and consecrated to thy name.

But will God indeed dwell on the earth? Behold, the heaven and heaven of heavens can not contain thee; how much less this house that we have built!

Yet have thou respect unto the **prayer of thy ser-**

vant, and to his supplication, O Lord my God, to hearken unto the cry and to the prayer of thy servant, and thy people,

That thine eyes may be open toward this house night and day, even toward the place consecrated to thy name.

And hearken thou to the supplication of thy servant, and of thy people; and hear thou in heaven thy dwelling-place; and when thou hearest, forgive.

For they be thy people, and thine inheritance. For thou didst separate them from among all the people of the earth to be thine inheritance.

Response by the Brethren.—The Lord is gracious, and his mercy endureth forever.

The Grand Chaplain then pronounces the following

BENEDICTION.

Blessed be the Lord that hath given rest unto his people. The Lord our God be with *us*, as he was with our *fathers;* let him not leave us, nor forsake us: that he may incline our hearts unto him, to walk in all his ways, and to keep his commandments, and his statutes, and his judgments, which he has commanded.

Response. — Glory be to God on high, on earth peace, good-will toward men.

The LODGE is then covered and the grand honors given, when the Grand Master retires to his chair.

The following ANTHEM is then sung:

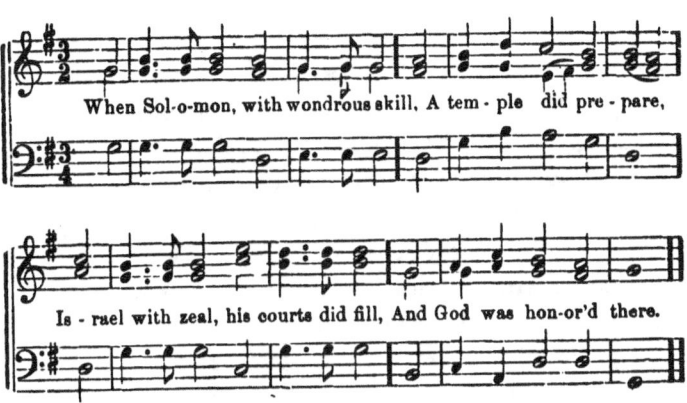

When Sol-o-mon, with wondrous skill, A tem - ple did pre - pare,

Is - rael with zeal, his courts did fill, And God was hon-or'd there.

When Solomon, with wond'rous skill,
 A temple did prepare,
Israel with zeal his courts did fill,
 And God was honor'd there.

Celestial rays of glorious light,
 The sacred walls contain'd ;
The pure refulgence, day and night,
 With awful force remain'd.

O may thy presence, gracious Lord,
 In our assembly be ;
Enlighten us to know thy Word,
 That we may honor Thee.

And when the final trump shall sound,
 To judge the world of sin,
Within thy courts may we be found,
 Eternally til'd in.

An address is then delivered, by some Brother appointed for
the occasion, after which the following ode is sung :

ODE.*

At dawn of creation, when bright beams of n﹐ ᴿing
  Broke through the regions of chaos and night,
And angels rejoic'd at the glory adorning
  The framework of nature with order and light;
     Soon as the brilliant ray,
     Symbol of endless day,
  Suffus'd with its blush the earth and the sea,
     Then on the new-born man
     Beam'd the grand mystic plan
Of Masonry's Orders, accepted and free.

From caves of old ocean, whose deep rolling fountair
  Gush where foundations of earth darkly lie,
Grand colums rise into ice-cover'd mountains,
  To prop up the arch of the star spangled sky.
     His was the shrine of love,
     Who, from His throne above,
  Ancient of days! gave the sovereign decree;
     And from the corner-stone
     Were all the virtues shown
Of Masonry's Orders, accepted and free.

A cherub there came of beauty in vision,
  Whom mortals have call'd by Faith's holy name;
Beside her next stood Hope, pure and elysian,
  As ever appear'd in the first dream of fame;
     And whilst immortals there,
     Charity, gracious fair!
  Daughter of heaven! burnt incense to thee;
     Swell'd anthems glorious!
     Triumph victorious!
Of Masonry's Orders, accepted and free.

* This ode, written by Brother St. John Phillips, M.D., was substituted by
the Grand Lodge of South Carolinain 1841, on the occasion of the dedication
of Masonic Hall in Charleston, for the one formerly used.

And here have we built, as a shelter from danger,
A temple to friendship and virtue combin'd,
Where the orphan, the widow, and destitute stranger,
A Mason's compassion and favor may find.
Far from deceit and art,
Freely with hand and heart,
Welcome the brother, whoever he be!
Here may the pilgrim guest
Find the sweet home of rest,
Of Masonry's Orders, accepted and free.

May the Grand Master whom, all things possessing,
The heaven of heavens can never contain,
Crown this good work with His favor and blessing,
And Charity's fabric in mercy sustain!
Till as the courses rise,
Up to the radiant skies,
In that Grand Lodge may all mankind agree;
And in the reign of peace,
Only with time shall cease
Great Masonry's Orders, accepted and free.

A collection is then made by the Grand Stewards, for the relief of distressed Masons, their widows and orphans. The grand procession is resumed, and after marching three times round the hall, *with the Lodge*, as at entrance, during which a grand piece of music is performed, the procession returns to the place whence it set out, where the laws of the Order are rehearsed, and the Grand Lodge is closed in ample form.

Note—When the distance is such that the Grand Master with his Grand officers can not conveniently attend, he may depute some skillful Past Master to represent him, who may call other worthy brethren to his assistance, and the form of proxy therefor is the same as that contained on page 124, for the Constitution of a Lodge, with the necessary verbal alterations.

SECTION VIII.

FUNERAL SERVICE.

O Freemason can be interred with the formalities of the Order, unless it be at his own request, or by that of some of his family, communicated to the Master of the Lodge of which he died a member (foreigners and transient brethren excepted) ; nor unless he has received the Master's degree ; and from this restriction there can be *no exception.* Fellow Crafts and Apprentices are not entitled to funeral obsequies ; nor to attend the Masonic processions on such occasions.

When the Master of a Lodge receives notice of a Master Mason's death, and of his request to be interred as a Mason, he must satisfy himself of its propriety ; and then, being informed of the time appointed for the funeral, the Master may invite as many Lodges as he may think proper, and the members of those Lodges may accompany their officers in form ; but the whole ceremony must be under the direction of the Master of the Lodge to which the deceased belonged, and he and his officers must be duly honored and cheerfully obeyed on the solemn occasion.

The brethren who walk in procession should observe, as much as possible, a uniformity in their dress. Decent mourning, with white stockings, gloves, and aprons, being the usual dress of Master Masons, is most suitable and becoming. No person should be distinguished with a jewel, unless he is an officer of one of the Lodges invited to attend ; and the officers of the Lodge to which the deceased belonged should wear sashes and hat-bands.

The brethren being assembled at the Lodge-room, or some other convenient place, the Master of the Lodge to which the deceased belonged opens the Lodge in the *third degree.* A procession is then formed to the house of the deceased, and thence to the grave in the following order, every brother carrying a sprig of evergreen:

Tiler, with a drawn sword;
The Stewards;
Master Masons;
Treasurer and Secretary;
Senior and Junior Wardens;
Past Masters;
The Bible, Square, and Compasses, on a blue velvet cushion, covered with black cloth, carried by the oldest member of the Lodge;
The Master, supported by two Deacons;
The Officiating Clergyman.

The Chief Mourner;
Other Mourners.

Before the procession begins, several of the brethren should proceed to the church-yard, to prevent confusion, and make the necessary preparations. The brethren are not to desert their ranks, nor change places, but keep in their proper order. When the procession arrives at the gate of the church-yard, the Lodge to which the deceased brother belonged, and the mourners and attendants on the corpse, halt, till the members of the other Lodges have formed a circle round the grave, when an opening is made to receive them. They then advance to the grave; when the clergyman and officers of the acting Lodge take their station at the head of the grave, and the mourners at the foot. After the clergyman has concluded the religious services of the church, the Masonic service begins.

CEREMONIES AT THE GRAVE.

Master. What man is he that liveth, and shall not see death? Shall he deliver his soul from the hand of the grave?

Response. Man walketh in a vain shadow, he heapeth up riches, and can not tell who shall gather them.

Master. He cometh forth like a flower, and is cut down: he fleeth also as a shadow, and continueth not.

Response. When he dieth he shall carry nothing away; his glory shall not descend after him.

Master. Naked came he into the world, and naked he must return.

Response. Man dieth and wasteth away; yea, man giveth up the ghost, and where is he?

Master. All flesh shall perish together, and man shall turn again unto dust.

Response. As the waters fail from the sea, and the flood decayeth and drieth up:

Master. So man lieth down and riseth not: till the heavens be no more they shall not awake, nor be raised out of their sleep.

Response. The Lord gave, and the Lord ha'h taken away, blessed be the name of the Lord.

Master. Let us die the death of the righteous, and let our last end be like his.

Response. God is our God forever and ever; he will be our guide even unto death!

Master. Almighty Father! into thy hands we commit the soul of our beloved brother.

The brethren answer three times, giving the grand honors each time:

The will of God is accomplished! So mote it be. Amen.

The Master then deposits the roll in the archives, and repeats the following

PRAYER.

Most glorious God! the Author of all good, and the giver of all mercy! pour down thy blessings upon us, and strengthen our most solemn engagements with the tie of sincere affection! May the present instance of mortality remind us of our approaching fate. May it draw our attention toward thee, the only refuge in time of need, that when the awful moment shall arrive in which we are about to leave this transitory scene the enlivening prospect of thy mercy may dispel the gloom and fear of death; that after our departure hence in peace, and in thy favor, we may be received into thine everlasting kingdom, and there enjoy, in union with the souls of our departed friends, the just reward of a pious and virtuous life. So mote it be. Amen.

The following exhortation is then given by the Master:

My brethren, here we view a striking instance of the uncertainty of life, and the vanity of all human pursuits. The last offices paid to the dead are only useful as lectures to the living; from them we are to derive instruction, and consider every solemnity of this kind as a summons to prepare for our own approaching dissolution.

Notwithstanding the various instances of mortality which we daily meet; notwithstanding death has established his empire over all the works of nature, yet, through some unaccountable infatuation, we forget that we are mortal; we forget that we are born to die. We go on from one design to another; we add hope to hope; we lay out plans for the employment of many years, until we are suddenly alarmed with the approach of death, when we least expect him, and at an hour when we probably think ourselves to be in the meridian of our existence.

What are all the pomp and splendor of majesty, the pride of wealth, or the charms of beauty, when nature has paid her just debt? Fix your eyes, my brethren, on the last scene; view life stripped of her ornaments, and exposed in her natural meanness; and you will then be convinced of the futility of all those empty delusions. In the grave, all fallacies are detected, all ranks are leveled, and all distinctions are done away.

While we drop the tear of sympathy over the grave of our deceased brother, let charity induce us to throw a vail over his frailties, whatever they may have been, and not withhold from his memory the praise that his virtues may have claimed. Suffer the apologies of human nature to plead in his behalf. Perfection on earth has never been attained by any human being. The wisest, as well as the best, of men have erred.

Let the present example excite our most serious thoughts, and strengthen our resolutions of amendment. As we see that life is uncertain, and that all earthly pursuits are vain, let us no longer postpone the important concern of preparing for eternity. Let us embrace the happy moment, while time and opportunity offer, to provide against the great change which we know must come, when all the pleasures of this world shall cease to delight, and the reflections of a religious and virtuous life will yield the only comfort and consolation. Thus our expectations will not be frustrated, nor we be hurried, unprepared, into the presence of an all-wise and powerful Judge, to whom the secrets of all hearts are known.

Let us, while in this state of probation, support with sincerity the character of our profession. Let us advert to the nature of our solemn ties, and pursue with assiduity the sacred tenets of our Order. Then, with becoming reverence, let us supplicate the divine grace to insure the favor of that Eternal Being whose goodness and power know no bound, that when the awful moment arrives, be it sooner or later, we may be enabled to prosecute our journey without dread or apprehension, to that undiscovered country whence no traveler returns.

The following invocations are then made by the Master, and the public grand honors accompany each response:

Master. May we be true and faithful; and may we live and die in love with our brother.

Brethren. So mote it be.

Master. May we profess what is good, and always act agreeably to our profession.

Brethren. So mote it be.

Master.—May the Lord bless us, and prosper us; and may all our good intentions be crowned with success.

Brethren. So mote it be.

The apron is then thrown into the grave, while the Master repeats, with an audible voice:

Glory be to God on high! on earth, peace, good-will to men!

Brethren. So mote it be, now, from henceforth, and for evermore.

The brethren march three times round the grave, casting therein their evergreens, and the public grand honors are then given   The Master closes with the following exhortation:

From time immemorial it has been a custom among the fraternity of Freemasons, at the request of a brother on his death-bed, or at the solicitation of his friends, to accompany his body to the place of interment, and there to deposit his remains with the usual formalities of our Order.

In conformity with this usage [and at the special request of our deceased brother, whose memory we revere, and whose loss we now deplore], we have assembled in the character of Freemasons, to resign his body to the earth whence it came [and to offer up to his memory before the world the last testimony of our regard]; thereby demonstrating [the sincerity of our past esteem, and] our inviolable attachment to the principles of the Order.*

The great Creator having been pleased, out of his wisdom and mercy, to remove our brother from the cares and troubles of a transitory existence to a state of eternal duration, and thereby to weaken the chain by which we are united, man to man, may we, who survive him, anticipate our approaching fate. May we be more strongly cemented in the ties of union and friendship; that during the short space allotted to our present existence and probation, we may wisely and usefully employ our time; and in the reciprocal intercourse of kind and friendly offices, mutually promote the welfare and happiness of each other, to the honor and glory of God, and the salvation of our own souls.

Unto the grave we have resigned the body of our deceased brother, there to remain until the general resurrection, in favorable expectation that his immortal soul may then partake of the joys which have been prepared for the righteous from the beginning of the world. And may Almighty God, of his infinite goodness, at the grand tribunal of unbiased justice, extend his mercy to him and all of us, and crown our hope with everlasting bliss in the realms of a

---

* What is included within brackets may be omitted in the case of transient brethren, or otherwise, as the officiating officer may think fit.

boundless eternity. This we beg for the honor of his name, to whom be glory now and forever. Amen.

Brethren. The will of God is accomplished. So mote it be. Amen.

Master. From dust we came, and unto dust we must return.

Brethren. May we all be recompensed at the resurrection of the just. Amen.

The procession then returns to the place whence it set out, where the necessary duties are complied with, and the business of Freemasonry is renewed. The insignia and ornaments of the deceased, if an officer of a Lodge, are returned to the Master, and the Lodge is closed in the third degree with the usual benediction.

When a Grand officer is interred, the service is performed by the Grand Chaplain, and the procession arranged according to the form of St. John's Day.

SECTION IX.

REGULATIONS FOR PROCESSIONS.

 HEN the Grand Master, Deputy Grand Master, or either of the Grand Wardens, joins the procession of a private Lodge, proper respect is to be paid to the rank of that officer. His position will be immediately before the Master and Wardens of the Lodge, and two Deacons will be appointed to attend him.

When the Grand or Deputy Grand Master is present, the Book of Constitutions will be borne before him. The honor of carrying this book belongs of right to the Master of the oldest Lodge in the jurisdiction, whenever he is present, in allusion to the fact that the Constitutions of the Order were originally vested in that officer, and that on him the business of the Grand Lodge devolves, in case of the absence of all the Grand officers, and also because it was a custom adopted soon after the reorganization of the Grand Lodge of England, for the Master of the oldest Lodge to attend every Grand Installation, and taking precedence of all others, the Grand Master only excepted, to deliver the Book of Constitutions to the newly installed Grand Master, thereby to remind him of his obligation to preserve the ancient landmarks and constitutions inviolate.

The Book of Constitutions must never be borne in a procession unless the Grand or Deputy Grand Master be present.

In entering public buildings, the Bible, Square, and Compasses, and the Book of Constitutions, are to be placed in front of the Grand Master, and the Grand Marshal and Grand Deacons must keep near him.

14

When a procession faces inward, the Deacons and Stewards will cross their rods, so as to form an arch for the brethren to pass beneath.

Marshals are to walk or ride on the left flank of a procession. The appropriate costume of a Marshal is a cocked hat, sword, and scarf, with a baton in his hand. The color of the scarf must be blue in the procession of a Subordinate Lodge, and purple in nat of the Grand Lodge.

All processions will return in the same order in which they set out.

The post of honor in a Masonic procession is always in the rear.

APPENDIXES

APPENDIX.

I.

THE TWENTY-FIVE LANDMARKS OF FREEMASONRY.*

THE modes of recognition.

II. The division of symbolic Masonry into three degrees.

III. The legend of the third degree.

IV. The government of the fraternity by a presiding officer called a *Grand Master*, who is elected from the body of the craft.

V. The prerogative of the Grand Master to preside over every assembly of the craft, wheresoever and whensoever held.

VI. The prerogative of the Grand Master to grant dispensations for conferring degrees at irregular times.

VII. The prerogative of the Grand Master to grant dispensations for opening and holding Lodges.

VIII. The prerogative of the Grand Master to make Masons at sight.

IX. The necessity for Masons to congregate in Lodges.

X. The government of every Lodge by a Master and two Wardens.

XI. The necessity that every Lodge, when congregated, should be duly tiled.

* A full explanation of and commentary on these Landmarks will be found in MACKEY's "Text-Book of Masonic Jurisprudence," pp. 17–89.

XII. The right of every Mason to be represented in all general meetings of the craft, and to instruct his representatives.

XIII. The right of every Mason to appeal from the decision of his brethren in Lodge convened to the Grand Lodge or General Assembly of Masons.

XIV. The right of every Mason to visit and sit in every regular Lodge.

XV. That no visitor, not known to some brother present as a Mason, can enter a Lodge without undergoing an examination.

XVI. That no Lodge can interfere in the business or labor of another Lodge.

XVII. That every Freemason is amenable to the laws and regulations of the Masonic jurisdiction in which he resides.

XVIII. That every candidate for initiation must be a man, free born and of lawful age.

XIX. That every Mason must believe in the existence of God as the Grand Architect of the Universe.

XX. That every Mason must believe in a resurrection to a future life.

XXI. That a book of the law of God must constitute an indispensable part of the furniture of every Lodge.

XXII. That all men in the sight of God are equal, and meet in the Lodge on one common level.

XXIII. That Freemasonry is a secret society, in possession of secrets that can not be divulged.

XXIV. That Freemasonry consists of a speculative science founded on an operative art.

XXV. That the Landmarks of Masonry can never be changed.

These constitute the Landmarks, or, as they have sometimes been called, "the body of Masonry," in which it is not in the power of any man, or body of men, to make the least innovation.

II.

Charges of a Freemason,

EXTRACTED from the Ancient Record of Lodges beyond sea, and of those in England, Scotland, and Ireland, for the use of the Lodges in London. To be read at the making of New Brethren, or when the Master shall order it.*

THE GENERAL HEADS, viz:

I. Of GOD and RELIGION.

II. Of the CIVIL MAGISTRATE, Supreme and Subordinate.

III. Of LODGES.

IV. Of MASTERS, WARDENS, FELLOWS, and APPRENTICES.

V. Of the Management of the CRAFT in working.

VI. Of BEHAVIOR, viz:

1. In the Lodge while CONSTITUTED.

2. After the Lodge is over and the BRETHREN not gone.

3. When Brethren meet without STRANGERS, but not in a LODGE.

4. In Presence of STRANGERS NOT MASONS.

5. At HOME and in the NEIGHBORHOOD.

6. Toward a STRANGE BROTHER.

I. CONCERNING GOD AND RELIGION.

A Mason is obliged, by his tenure, to obey the moral law, and if he rightly understands the art, he will never be a stupid

* NOTE BY THE EDITOR.—These charges were prepared and presented to the Grand Lodge of England in 1721 by Dr. ANDERSON and Dr DESAGULIERS, and having been approved by the Grand Lodge on the 25th of March, 1722, were published in the first edition of the Book of Constitutions. They have always been held in the highest veneration by the fraternity, as embodying the most important points of the ancient written, as well as unwritten, law of Masonry

atheist nor an irreligious libertine. But though in ancient times Masons were charged in every country to be of the religion of that country or nation, whatever it was, it is now thought more expedient only to oblige them to that religion in which all men agree, leaving their particular opinions to themselves; that is, to be *good men and true*, or men of honor and honesty, by whatever denominations or persuasions they may be distinguished whereby Masonry becomes the *center of union*, and the means of conciliating true friendship among persons that must have remained at a perpetual distance.

II. OF THE CIVIL MAGISTRATE, SUPREME AND SUBORDINATE.

A Mason is a peaceable subject to the civil powers wherever he resides or works, and is never to be concerned in plots and conspiracies against the peace and welfare of the nation, nor to behave himself undutifully to inferior magistrates; for as Masonry hath always been injured by war, bloodshed, and confusion, so ancient kings and princes have been much disposed to encourage the craftsmen, because of their peaceableness and loyalty, whereby they practically answered the cavils of their adversaries, and promoted the honor of the fraternity, who ever flourished in times of peace. So that if a brother should be a rebel against the state, he is not to be countenanced in his rebellion, however he may be pitied as an unhappy man; and, if convicted of no other crime, though the loyal brotherhood must and ought to disown his rebellion, and give no umbrage or ground of political jealousy to the government for the time being, they can not expel him from the Lodge, and his relation to it remains indefeasible.

III. OF LODGES.

A Lodge is a place where Masons assemble and work; hence that assembly, or duly organized society of Masons, is called a *Lodge*, and every brother ought to belong to one, and to be subject to its by-laws and the General Regulations. It is either particular or general, and will be best understood by attending it, and by the regulations of the General or Grand Lodge hereunto annexed. In ancient times, no Master or Fellow could be absent from it, especially when warned to appear at it, without incurring a severe censure, until it appeared to the Master and Wardens that pure necessity hindered him.

The persons admitted members of a Lodge must be good and true men, free-born, and of mature and discreet age, no bond men, no women, no immoral or scandalous men, but of good report.

IV. OF MASTERS, WARDENS, FELLOWS, AND APPRENTICES.

All preferment among Masons is grounded upon real worth and personal merit only; that so the lords may be well served, the brethren not put to shame, nor the Royal Craft despised: Therefore no Master or Warden is chosen by seniority, but for his merit. It is impossible to describe these things in writing, and every brother must attend in his place, and learn them in a way peculiar to this fraternity: only candidates may know that no Master should take an Apprentice unless he has sufficient employment for him, and unless he be a perfect youth, having no maim or defect in his body, that may render him uncapable of learning the art of serving his Master's LORD, and of being made a *Brother*, and then a *Fellow Craft* in due time, even after he has served such a term of years as the custom of the country directs; and that he should be descended of honest parents; that so, when otherwise qualified, he may arrive at the honor of being the *Warden*, and then the *Master* of the Lodge, the *Grand Warden*, and at length the *Grand Master* of all the Lodges, according to his merit.

No brother can be a Warden until he has passed the part of a Fellow Craft; nor a Master until he has acted as a Warden, nor Grand Warden until he has been Master of a Lodge, nor GRAND MASTER unless he has been a Fellow Craft before his election, who is also to be nobly born, or a gentleman of the best fashion, or some eminent scholar, or some curious architect, or other artist, descended of honest parents, and who is of singular great merit in the opinion of the Lodges. And for the better, and easier, and more honorable discharge of his office, the Grand Master has a power to choose his own Deputy Grand Master, who must be then, or must have been formerly, the Master of a particular Lodge, and has the privilege of acting whatever the Grand Master, his principal, should act, unless the said principal be present, or interpose his authority by a letter.

These rulers and governors, supreme and subordinate, of the ancient Lodge, are to be obeyed in their respective stations by all the brethren, according to the Old Charges and regulations, with all humility, reverence, love, and alacrity.

V. OF THE MANAGEMENT OF THE CRAFT IN WORKING.

All Masons shall work honestly on working days, that they may live creditably on holy days; and the time appointed by the law of the land, or confirmed by custom, shall be observed.

The most expert of the Fellow Craftsmen shall be chosen or appointed the Master, or Overseer, of the lord's work; who is to be called *Master* by those that work under him. The Craftsmen are to avoid all ill language, and to call each other by no disobliging name, but brother or fellow; and to behave themselves courteously within and without the Lodge.

The Master knowing himself to be able of cunning, shall under-take the lord's work as reasonably as possible, and truly dispend his goods as if they were his own; nor to give more wages to any brother or apprentice than he really may deserve.

Both the Master and the Masons receiving their wages justly, shall be faithful to the lord, and honestly finish their work, whether task or journey; nor put the work to task that hath been accustomed to journey.

None shall discover envy at the prosperity of a brother, nor supplant him, or put him out of his work, if he be capable to finish the same; for no man can finish another's work so much to the lord's profit, unless he be thoroughly acquainted with the designs and draughts of him that began it.

When a Fellow Craftsman is chosen Warden of the work under the Master, he shall be true both to Master and fellows, shall carefully oversee the work in the Master's absence to the lord's profit; and his brethren shall obey him.

All Masons employed shall meekly receive their wages without murmuring or mutiny, and not desert the Master till the work is finished.

A younger brother shall be instructed in working, to prevent spoiling the materials for want of judgment, and for increasing and continuing of brotherly love.

All the tools used in working shall be approved by the Grand Lodge.

No laborer shall be employed in the proper work of Masonry; nor shall Freemasons work with those that are not free, without an urgent necessity; nor shall they teach laborers and unaccepted Masons, as they should teach a brother or fellow.

VI. OF BEHAVIOR, VIZ:

1. IN THE LODGE WHILE CONSTITUTED.

You are not to hold private committees, or separate conversation, without leave from the Master, nor to talk of anything impertinent or unseemly, nor interrupt the Master or Wardens, or any brother speaking to the Master; nor behave yourself ludicrously or jestingly while the Lodge is engaged in what is serious and solemn; nor use any unbecoming language upon any pretense whatsoever; but to pay due reverence to your Master, Wardens, and Fellows, and put them to worship.

If any complaint be brought, the brother found guilty shall stand to the award and determination of the Lodge, who are the proper and competent judges of all such controversies (unless you carry it by appeal to the Grand Lodge), and to whom they ought to be referred, unless a lord's work be hindered the meanwhile, in which case a particular reference may be made; but you must never go to law about what concerneth *Masonry*, without an absolute necessity apparent to the Lodge.

2. BEHAVIOR AFTER THE LODGE IS OVER AND THE BRETHREN NOT GONE.

You may enjoy yourselves with innocent mirth, treating one another according to ability, but avoiding all excess, or forcing any brother to eat or drink beyond his inclination, or hindering him from going when his occasions call him, or doing or saying anything offensive, or that may forbid an *easy* and *free* conversation; for that would blast our harmony and defeat our laudable purposes. Therefore no private piques or quarrels must be brought within the door of the Lodge, far less any quarrels about religion, or nations, or state policy, we being only, as Masons. of the catholic religion above-mentioned; we are also of all nations, tongues, kindreds, and languages, and are resolved against *all politics*, as what never yet conduced to the welfare of the Lodge, nor ever will. This *Charge* has been always strictly enjoined and observed; but especially ever since the Reformation in Britain, or the dissent and secession of these nations from the communion of Rome.

3. BEHAVIOR WHEN BRETHREN MEET WITHOUT STRANGERS, BUT NOT IN A LODGE FORMED.

You are to salute one another in a courteous manner, as you will be instructed, calling each other *Brother*, freely giving mutual instruction as shall be thought expedient, without being overseen or overheard, and without encroaching upon each other, or derogating from that respect which is due to any brother, were he not a Mason; for though all Masons are as brethren upon the same level, yet Masonry takes no honor from a man that he had before; nay, rather it adds to his honor, especially if he has deserved well of the brotherhood, who must give honor to whom it is due, and avoid ill manners.

4. BEHAVIOR IN PRESENCE OF STRANGERS NOT MASONS.

You shall be cautious in your words and carriage, that the most penetrating stranger shall not be able to discover or find out what is not proper to be intimated; and sometimes you shall divert a discourse, and manage it prudently for the honor of the Worshipful Fraternity.

5. BEHAVIOR AT HOME, AND IN YOUR NEIGHBORHOOD.

You are to act as becomes a moral and wise man; particularly, not to let your family, friends, and neighbors know the

concerns of the Lodge, etc., but wisely to consult your own
honor, and that of the Ancient Brotherhood, for reasons not to
be mentioned here. You must also consult your health by not
continuing together too late, or too long from home, after Lodge
hours are past; and by avoiding of gluttony or drunkenness,
that your families be not neglected or injured, nor you disabled
from working.

6. BEHAVIOR TOWARD A STRANGE BROTHER.

You are cautiously to examine him, in such a method as pru
dence shall direct you, that you may not be imposed upon by an
ignorant false pretender, whom you are to reject with contempt
and derision, and beware of giving him any hints of knowledge.

But if you discover him to be a true and genuine brother, you
are to respect him accordingly; and if he is in want, you must
relieve him if you can, or else direct him how he may be relieved;
you must employ him some days, or else recommend him to be
employed. But you are not charged to do beyond your ability,
only to prefer a poor brother, that is a good man and true,
before any other poor people in the same circumstances.

Finally, All these CHARGES you are to observe, and also those
that shall be communicated to you in another way; cultivating
brotherly love, the foundation and cap-stone, the cement and
glory, of this ancient fraternity, avoiding all wrangling and quar-
reling, all slander and backbiting, nor permitting others to slander any honest brother, but defending his character, and doing
him all good offices, as far as is consistent with your honor and
safety, and no further. And if any of them do you injury, you
must apply to your own or his Lodge; and from thence you may
appeal to the Grand Lodge at the quarterly communication, and
from thence to the annual Grand Lodge, as has been the ancient
laudable conduct of our forefathers in every nation; never
taking a legal course, but when the case can not be otherwise
decided, and patiently listening to the honest and friendly
advice of Master and fellows when they would prevent you going
to law with strangers, or would excite you to put a speedy period

to all law-suits, that so you may mind the affair of Masonry with the more alacrity and success; but with respect to brothers or fellows at law, the Master and brethren should kindly offer their mediation, which ought to be thankfully submitted to by the contending brethren; and if that submission is impracticable, they must, however, carry on their process or law-suit without wrath and rancor (not in the common way), saying or doing nothing which may hinder brotherly love, and good offices to be renewed and continued; that all may see the benign influence of Masonry, as all true Masons have done from the beginning of the world and will do to the end of time.

Amen. So mote it be.

III.

General Regulations,*

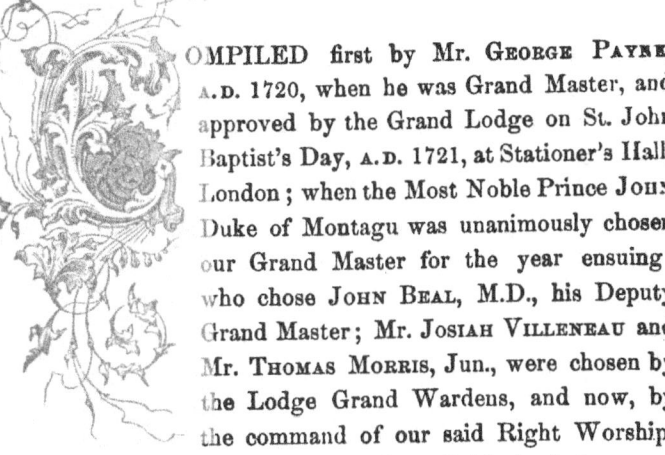OMPILED first by Mr. GEORGE PAYNE, A.D. 1720, when he was Grand Master, and approved by the Grand Lodge on St. John Baptist's Day, A.D. 1721, at Stationer's Hall, London; when the Most Noble Prince JOHN Duke of Montagu was unanimously chosen our Grand Master for the year ensuing; who chose JOHN BEAL, M.D., his Deputy Grand Master; Mr. JOSIAH VILLENEAU and Mr. THOMAS MORRIS, Jun., were chosen by the Lodge Grand Wardens, and now, by the command of our said Right Worship-ful Grand Master MONTAGU, the author of this book has com-pared them with, and reduced them to the ancient records and immemorial usages of the fraternity, and digested them into this new method, with several proper explications, for the use of the Lodges in and about London and Westminster.

I. The Grand Master, or his Deputy, hath authority and right not only to be present in any true Lodge, but also to preside wherever he is, with the Master of the Lodge on his left hand, and to order his Grand Wardens to attend him, who are not to act in particular Lodges as Wardens but in his presence and at his command; because there the Grand Master may command

---

* NOTE BY THE EDITOR.—The most complete history that could be given of these Regulations is to be found in their title. Adopted by the Grand Lodge of England soon after its organization, they are entitled to great respect, although not of equal authority either with the Landmarks, the Old Charges, or the local Regulations of any Grand Lodge which may have changed them in the formal manner which these Regulations themselves prescribe

the Wardens of that Lodge, or any other brethren he pleaseth to attend and act as his Wardens *pro tempore*.

II. The Master of a particular Lodge has the right and author-ity of congregating the members of his Lodge into a Chapter at pleasure, upon any emergency or occurrence, as well as to appoint the time and place of their usual forming; and in case of sick-ness, death, or necessary absence of the Master, the Senior Warden shall act as Master *pro tempore*, if no brother is present who has been Master of that Lodge before; for in that case the absent Master's authority reverts to the last Master then present; though he can not act until the said Senior Warden has once congregated the Lodge, or, in his absence, the Junior Warden.

III. The Master of each particular Lodge, or one of the Wardens, or some other brother by his order, shall keep a book containing their by-laws, the names of their members, with a list of all the Lodges in town, and the usual times and places of their forming, and all their transactions that are proper to be written.

IV. No Lodge shall make more than five new brethren at one time, nor any man under the age of twenty-five, who must be also his own master; unless by a dispensation from the Grand Master or his Deputy.

V. No man can be made or admitted a member of a particular Lodge without previous notice one month before given to the said Lodge, in order to make due inquiry into the reputation and capacity of the candidate, unless by the dispensation aforesaid.

VI. But no man can be entered a brother in any particular Lodge, or admitted to be a member thereof, without the unani-mous consent of all the members of that Lodge then present when the candidate is proposed, and their consent is formally asked by the Master; and they are to signify their consent or dissent in their own prudent way, either virtually or in form, but with unanimity: nor is this inherent privilege subject to a dispensation; because the members of a particular Lodge are the best judges of it; and if a fractious member should be imposed on them, it might spoil their harmony or hinder their freedom.

or even break or disperse the Lodge; which ought to be avoided by all good and true brethren.

VII. Every new brother at his making is decently to clothe the Lodge, that is, all the brethren present, and to deposit something for the relief of indigent and decayed brethren, as the candidate shall think fit to bestow, over and above the small allowance stated by the by-laws of that particular Lodge; which charity shall be lodged with the Master or Wardens, or the Cashier, if the members think fit to choose one.

And the candidate shall also solemnly promise to submit to the Constitutions, the Charges, and Regulations, and to such other good usages as shall be intimated to him in time and place convenient.

VIII. No set or number of brethren shall withdraw or separate themselves from the Lodge in which they were made brethren, or were afterward admitted members, unless the Lodge becomes too numerous; nor even then, without a dispensation from the Grand Master or his Deputy; and when they are thus separated, they must either immediately join themselves to such other Lodge as they shall like best, with the unanimous consent of that other Lodge to which they go (as above regulated), or else they must obtain the Grand Master's Warrant to join in forming a new Lodge.

If any set or number of Masons shall take upon themselves to form a Lodge without the Grand Master's Warrant, the regular Lodges are not to countenance them, nor own them as fair brethren and duly formed, nor approve of their acts and deeds; but must treat them as rebels, until they humble themselves, as the Grand Master shall in his prudence direct, and until he approve of them by his Warrant, which must be signified to the other Lodges, as the custom is when a new Lodge is to be registered in the list of Lodges.

IX. But if any brother so far misbehaves himself as to render his Lodge uneasy, he shall be twice duly admonished by the Master or Wardens in a formed Lodge; and if he will not refrain his imprudence, and obediently submit to the advice of the brethren, and reform what gives them offense, he shall be dealt with according to the by-laws of that particular Lodge, or else in such a manner as the quarterly communication shall in their great prudence think fit; for which a new regulation may be afterward made.

X. The majority of every particular Lodge, when congregated, shall have the privilege of giving instructions to their Master and Wardens before the assembling of the Grand Chapter, or Lodge, at the three quarterly communications hereafter mentioned, and of the annual Grand Lodge too; because their Masters and Wardens are their representatives, and are supposed to speak their mind.

XI. All particular Lodges are to observe the same usages as much as possible; in order to which, and for cultivating a good understanding among Freemasons, some members out of every Lodge shall be deputed to visit the other Lodges as often as shall be thought convenient.

XII. The Grand Lodge consists of, and is formed by, the Masters and Wardens of all the regular particular Lodges upon record, with the Grand Master at their head, and his Deputy on his left hand, and the Grand Wardens in their proper places, and must have a quarterly communication about Michaelmas, Christmas, and Lady Day, in some convenient place, as the Grand Master shall appoint, where no brother shall be present who is not at that time a member thereof, without a dispensation; and while he stays, he shall not be allowed to vote, nor even give his opinion, without leave of the Grand Lodge asked and given, or unless it be duly asked by the said Lodge.

All matters are to be determined in the Grand Lodge by a majority of votes, each member having one vote, and the Grand Master having two votes, unless the said Lodge leave any particular thing to the determination of the Grand Master for the sake of expedition.

XIII. At the said quarterly communication, all matters that concern the fraternity in general, or particular Lodges, or single brethren, are quietly, sedately, and maturely to be discoursed of and transacted: Apprentices must be admitted Masters and Fellow Craft only here, unless by a dispensation. Here also all differences that can not be made up and accommodated privately, nor by a particular Lodge, are to be seriously considered and decided: and if any brother thinks himself aggrieved by the decision of this board, he may appeal to the annual Grand Lodge next ensuing, and leave his appeal in writing with the Grand Master, or his Deputy, or the Grand Wardens.

Here also the Master or the Wardens of each particular Lodge shall bring and produce a list of such members as have been made, or even admitted in their particular Lodges since the last communication of the Grand Lodge: and there shall be a book kept by the Grand Master, or his Deputy, or rather by some brother whom the Grand Lodge shall appoint for Secretary, wherein shall be recorded all the Lodges, with their usual times and places of forming, and the names of all the members of each Lodge; and all the affairs of the Grand Lodge that are proper to be written.

They shall also consider of the most prudent and effectual methods of collecting and disposing of what money shall be given to, or lodged with them in charity, toward the relief only of any true brother fallen into poverty or decay, but of none else: but every particular Lodge shall dispose of their own charity for poor brethren according to their own by-laws, until it be agreed by all the Lodges (in a new regulation) to carry in the charity collected by them to the Grand Lodge at the quarterly or annual communication, in order to make a common stock of it, for the more handsome relief of poor brethren.

They shall also appoint a Treasurer, a brother of good worldly substance, who shall be a member of the Grand Lodge by virtue of his office, and shall be always present, and have power to move to the Grand Lodge anything, especially what concerns his office. To him shall be committed all money raised for charity, or for any other use of the Grand Lodge, which he shall write down in a book, with the respective ends and uses for which the several sums are intended; and shall expend and disburse the same by such a certain order, signed, as the Grand Lodge shall afterward agree to in a new regulation; but he shall not vote in choosing a Grand Master or Wardens, though in every other transaction.   As in like manner the Secretary shall be a member of the Grand Lodge by virtue of his office, and vote in everything except in choosing a Grand Master or Wardens.

The Treasurer and Secretary shall have each a clerk, who must be a brother and Fellow Craft, but never must be a member of the Grand Lodge, nor speak without being allowed or desired.

The Grand Master, or his Deputy, shall always command the Treasurer and Secretary, with their clerks and books, in order to see how matters go on, and to know what is expedient to be done upon any emergent occasion.

Another brother (who must be a Fellow Craft) should be appointed to look after the door of the Grand Lodge; but shall be no member of it.

But these offices may be further explained by a new regulation, when the necessity and expediency of them may more appear than at present to the fraternity.

XIV. If at any Grand Lodge, stated or occasional, quarterly or annual, the Grand Master and his Deputy should be both absent, then the present Master of a Lodge that has been the longest a Freemason, shall take the chair and preside as Grand Master *pro tempore*, and shall be vested with all his power and honor for the time; provided there is no brother present that has been Grand Master formerly, or Deputy Grand Master; for the last Grand Master present, or else the last Deputy present, should always of right take place in the absence of the present Grand Master and his Deputy.

XV. In the Grand Lodge none can act as Wardens but the Grand Wardens themselves, if present; and if absent, the Grand Master, or the person who presides in his place, shall order private Wardens to act as Grand Wardens *pro tempore*, whose places are to be supplied by two Fellow Craft of the same Lodge, called forth to act, or sent thither by the particular Master thereof; or if by him omitted, then they shall be called by the Grand Master, that so the Grand Lodge may be always complete.

XVI. The Grand Wardens, or any others, are first to advise with the Deputy about the affairs of the Lodge or of the breth-

ren, and no; to apply to the Grand Master without the knowledge of the Deputy, unless he refuse his concurrence in any
certain necessary affair; in which case, or in case of any difference between the Deputy and the Grand Wardens, or other
brethren, both parties are to go by concert to the Grand Master,
who can easily decide the controversy and make up the differ
ance by virtue of his great authority.

The Grand Master should receive no intimation of business
concerning Masonry but from his Deputy first, except in such
certain cases as his Worship can well judge of; for if the application to the Grand Master be irregular, he can easily order the
Grand Wardens, or any other brethren thus applying, to wait
upon his Deputy, who is to prepare the business speedily, and to
lay it orderly before his Worship.

XVII. No Grand Master, Deputy Grand Master, Grand
Wardens, Treasurer, Secretary, or whoever acts for them, or in
their stead *pro tempore*, can at the same time be the Master or
Warden of a particular Lodge; but as soon as any of them has
honorably discharged his Grand office, he returns to that post or
station in his particular Lodge from which he was called to
officiate above.

XVIII. If the Deputy Grand Master be sick, or necessarily
absent, the Grand Master may choose any Fellow Craft he please
to be his Deputy *pro tempore;* but he that is chosen Deputy at
the Grand Lodge, and the Grand Wardens too, can not be discharged without the cause fairly appear to the majority of the
Grand Lodge; and the Grand Master, if he is uneasy, may call
a Grand Lodge on purpose to lay the cause before them, and
to have their advice and concurrence; in which case, the majority
of the Grand Lodge, if they can not reconcile the Master and his
Deputy or his Wardens, are to concur in allowing the Master to
discharge his said Deputy or his said Wardens, and to choose
another Deputy immediately; and the said Grand Lodge shall
choose other Wardens in that case, that harmony and peace may
be preserved.

XIX. If the Grand Master should abuse his power, and render
himself unworthy of the obedience and subjection of the Lodges,

he shall be treated in a way and manner to be agreed upon in a new regulation; because hitherto the ancient fraternity have had no occasion for it, their former Grand Masters having all behaved themselves worthy of that honorable office.

XX. The Grand Master, with his Deputy and Wardens, shall (at least once) go round and visit all the Lodges about town during his Mastership.

XXI. If the Grand Master die during his Mastership, or by sickness, or by being beyond sea, or any other way should be rendered incapable of discharging his office, the Deputy, or, in his absence, the Senior Grand Warden, or, in his absence, the Junior, or, in his absence, any three present Masters of Lodges, shall join to congregate the Grand Lodge immediately, to advise together upon that emergency, and to send two of their number to invite the last Grand Master to resume his office, which now in course reverts to him; or, if he refuse, then the next last, and so backward. But if no former Grand Master can be found, then the Deputy shall act as principal until another is chosen; or if there be no Deputy, then the oldest Master.

XXII. The brethren of all the Lodges in and about London and Westminster shall meet at an annual communication and feast, in some convenient place, on St. John Baptist's Day, or else on St. John Evangelist's Day, as the Grand Lodge shall think fit by a new regulation, having of late years met on St. John Baptist's Day: Provided,

The majority of the Masters and Wardens, with the Grand Master, his Deputy, and Wardens, agree at their quarterly communications, three months before, that there shall be a feast and a general communication of all the brethren; for if either the Grand Master, or the majority of the particular Masters, are against it, it must be dropped for that time.

But whether there shall be a feast for all the brethren or not, yet the Grand Lodge must meet in some convenient place annually on St. John's Day; or if it be Sunday, then on the next day, in order to choose every year a new Grand Master, Deputy, and Wardens.

XXIII. If it be thought expedient, and the Grand Master,

with the majority of the Masters and Wardens, agree to hold a grand feast, according to the ancient laudable custom of Masons, then the Grand Wardens shall have the care of preparing the tickets, sealed with the Grand Master's seal, of disposing of the tickets, of receiving the money for the tickets, of buying the materials of the feast, of finding out a proper and convenient place to feast in, and of every other thing that concerns the entertainment.

But, that the work may not be too burdensome to the two Grand Wardens, and that all matters may be expeditiously and safely managed, the Grand Master, or his Deputy, shall have power to nominate and appoint a certain number of Stewards, as his Worship shall think fit, to act in concert with the two Grand Wardens; all things relating to the feast being decided among them by a majority of voices, except the Grand Master or his Deputy interpose by a particular direction or appointment.

XXIV. The Wardens and Stewards shall, in due time, wait upon the Grand Master, or his Deputy, for directions and orders about the premises; but if his Worship and his Deputy are sick, or necessarily absent, they shall call together the Masters and Wardens of Lodges to meet on purpose for their advice and orders; or else they may take the matter wholly upon themselves, and do the best they can.

The Grand Wardens and the Stewards are to account for all the money they receive, or expend, to the Grand Lodge, after dinner, or when the Grand Lodge shall think fit to receive their accounts.

If the Grand Master pleases, he may in due time summon all the Masters and Wardens of Lodges, to consult with them about ordering the grand feast, and about any emergency or accidental thing relating thereunto, that may require advice; or else to take it upon himself altogether.

XXV. The Masters of Lodges shall each appoint one experienced and discreet Fellow Craft of his Lodge, to compose a committee, consisting of one from every Lodge, who shall meet to receive, in a convenient apartment, every person that brings a ticket, and shall have power to discourse him, if they think fit, in order to admit him or debar him, as they shall see cause Provided they send no man away before they have acquainted all the brethren within doors with the reasons thereof, to avoid mistakes; that so no true brother may be debarred, nor a false brother or mere pretender admitted. This committee must meet very early on St. John's Day at the place, even before any persons come with tickets.

XXVI. The Grand Master shall appoint two or more trusty brethren to be porters or doorkeepers, who are also to be early at the place, for some good reasons; and who are to be at the command of the committee.

XXVII. The Grand Wardens, or the Stewards, shall appoint beforehand such a number of brethren to serve at table as they think fit and proper for that work: and they may advise with the Masters and Wardens of Lodges about the most proper persons, if they please, or may take in such by their recommendation; for none are to serve that day but Free and Accepted Masons, that the communications may be free and harmonious.

XXVIII. All the members of the Grand Lodge must be at the place long before dinner, with the Grand Master, or his Deputy, at their head, who shall retire and form themselves. And this is done in order—

1. To receive any appeals duly lodged, as above regulated, that the appellant may be heard, and the affair may be amicably decided before dinner, if possible; but if it can not, it must be delayed till after the new Grand Master is elected; and if it can not be decided after dinner, it may be delayed, and referred to a particular committee, that shall quietly adjust it, and make report to the next quarterly communication, that brotherly love may be preserved.

2. To prevent any difference or disgust which may be feared to arise that day, that no interruption may be given to the harmony and pleasure of the Grand feast.

3. To consult about whatever concerns the decency and decorum of the Grand assembly, and to prevent all indecency and ill manners, the assembly being promiscuous.

4. To receive and consider of any good motion, or any mo

ˈuentous and important affair that shall be brought from the particular Lodges by their representatives, the several Masters and Wardens.

XXIX. After these things are discussed, the Grand Master and his Deputy, the Grand Wardens, or the Stewards, the Secretary, the Treasurer, the Clerks, and every other person shall withdraw and leave the Masters and Wardens of the particular Lodges alone, in order to consult amicably about electing a new Grand Master, or continuing the present, if they have not done it the day before; and if they are unanimous for continuing the present Grand Master, his Worship shall be called in, and humbly desired to do the fraternity the honor of ruling them for the year ensuing; and after dinner it will be known whether he accepts of it or not; for it should not be discovered but by the election itself.

XXX. Then the Masters and Wardens, and all the brethren, may converse promiscuously, or as they please to sort together, until the dinner is coming in, when every brother takes his seat at table.

XXXI. Some time after dinner, the Grand Lodge is formed, not in the retirement, but in the presence of all the brethren who yet are not members of it, and must not therefore speak until they are desired and allowed.

XXXII. If the Grand Master of last year has consented with the Master and Wardens in private, before dinner, to continue for the year ensuing, then one of the Grand Lodge, deputed for that purpose, shall represent to all the brethren his Worship's good government, etc., and, turning to him, shall, in the name of the Grand Lodge, humbly request him to do the fraternity the great honor (if nobly born, if not), the great kindness, of continuing to be their Grand Master for the year ensuing. And his Worship declaring his consent by a bow or a speech, as he pleases, the said deputed member of the Grand Lodge shall proclaim him Grand Master, and all the members of the Lodge shall salute him in due form. And all the brethren shall for a few minutes have leave to declare their satisfaction, pleasure, and congratulation.

XXXIII. But if either the Master and Wardens have not in private, this day before dinner, nor the day before, desired the last Grand Master to continue in the Mastership another year; or if he, when desired, has not consented: Then

The last Grand Master shall nominate his successor for the year ensuing, who, if unanimously approved by the Grand Lodge, and if there present, shall be proclaimed, saluted, and congratulated the new Grand Master as above hinted, and immediately installed by the last Grand Master according to usage.

XXXIV. But if that nomination is not unanimously approved, the new Grand Master shall be chosen immediately by ballot, every Master and Warden writing his man's name, and the last Grand Master writing his man's name too; and the man whose name the last Grand Master shall first take out, casually or by chance, shall be Grand Master for the year ensuing; and, if present, he shall be proclaimed, saluted, and congratulated, as above hinted, and forthwith installed by the last Grand Master, according to usage.

XXXV. The last Grand Master thus continued, or the new Grand Master thus installed, shall next nominate and appoint his Deputy Grand Master, either the last or a new one, who shall be also declared, saluted, and congratulated, as above hinted.

The Grand Master shall also nominate the new Grand Wardens, and, if unanimously approved by the Grand Lodge, shall be declared, saluted, and congratulated, as above hinted; but if not, they shall be chosen by ballot, in the same way as the Grand Master; as the Wardens of private Lodges are also to be chosen by ballot in each Lodge, if the members thereof do not agree to their Master's nomination.

XXXVI. But if the brother whom the present Grand Master shall nominate for his successor, or whom the majority of the Grand Lodge shall happen to chose by ballot, is, by sickness or other necessary occasion, absent from the Grand feast, he can not be proclaimed the new Grand Master, unless the old Grand Master, or some of the Masters and Wardens of the Grand Lodge can vouch, upon the honor of a brother, that the said person so nominated or chosen will readily accept of the said office; in which case the old Grand Master shall act as proxy, and shall nominate the Deputy and Wardens in his name, and in his name also receive the usual honors, homage, and congratulation.

XXXVII. Then the Grand Master shall allow any brother Fellow Craft, or Apprentice to speak, directing his discourse to nis Worship; or to make any motion for the good of the fraternity, which shall be either immediately considered and finished, or else referred to the consideration of the Grand Lodge at their next communication, stated or occasional. When that is over,

XXXVIII. The Grand Master or his Deputy, or some brother appointed by him, shall harangue all the brethren, and give them good advice; and lastly, after some other transactions, that can not be written in any language, the brethren may go away or stay longer, as they please.

XXXIX. Every annual Grand Lodge has an inherent power and authority to make new Regulations, or to alter these, for the real benefit of this ancient fraternity: Provided always that the old Landmarks be carefully preserved, and that such alterations and new Regulations be proposed and agreed to at the third quarterly communication preceding the annual Grand feast; and that they be offered also to the perusal of all the brethren before dinner, in writing, even of the youngest Apprentice, the approbation and consent of the majority of all the brethren present being absolutely necessary to make the same binding and obligatory; which must, after dinner, and after the new Grand Master is installed, be solemnly desired; as it was desired and obtained for these Regulations, when proposed by the Grand Lodge, to about 150 brethren, on St. John Baptist's Day, 1721.

IV.

Forms of Documents.

1 PETITION TO THE GRAND MASTER FOR A DISPENSA
TION TO OPEN AND HOLD A LODGE.

THE petition of the undersigned respectfully showeth, that
they are regular Freemasons, and are at present or have been
members of regular Lodges, that having the prosperity of the
fraternity at heart, they are willing to exert their best endeavors
to promote and diffuse the genuine principles of Freemasonry;
that for the conveniency of their respective dwellings [other
wise, stating the circumstances of the case], and for other good
reasons, they have agreed to form a new Lodge; that in consequence of this resolution, they pray the Most Worshipful Grand
Master for a dispensation to empower them to assemble as a
regular Lodge at .... and there to discharge the duties of
Freemasonry in a regular and constitutional manner, according
to the ancient usages of the Order, and the rules and regulations
of the Grand Lodge of Ancient Freemasons of ....;
that they have nominated and do recommend A. B. to be the
first Master, and C. D. to be the first Senior Warder, and E. F.
the first Junior Warden of the said Lodge: and the prayer of
this petition being granted, they promise strict conformity to
every regular edict and command of the Grand Master, and to
the constitutions, laws, and regulations of the Grand Lodge of
ancient Freemasons of ....

This petition must be signed by, at least, seven regular Master Masons,
and be recommended by the nearest Lodge, and be delivered to the Grand
Secretary, who shall present it to the Grand Master, or, in his absence to
the Deputy Grand Master.

11 DISPENSATION OF THE GRAND MASTER TO OPEN AND HOLD A LODGE.

To all whom it may concern:

WHEREAS, we ...... Most Worshipful Grand Master of Ancient Freemasons of ...., have received a petition from a constitutional number of brethren who have been regularly vouched for and recommended, which petition sets forth that they are desirous of establishing a new Lodge at .... under our Masonic jurisdiction, and requesting a dispensation for the same; and whereas there appears to us good and sufficient cause for granting the prayer of the said petition—

Now know ye, that we, the Most Worshipful Grand Master aforesaid, by virtue of the powers in us vested by the Ancient Constitutions of the Order, do hereby grant this our dispensation, authorizing and empowering Brother ...... to act as Worshipful Master, Brother ...... to act as Senior Warden, and Brother ...... to act as Junior Warden of a Lodge, to be held under our jurisdiction at ......, and to be known as .... Lodge. And we further authorize and empower the said brethren to *Enter, Pass,* and *Raise* Freemasons according to the Ancient Constitutions of the Order, the customs and usages of the craft, and the rules and regulations of the Grand Lodge of Ancient Freemasons of ...., and not otherwise. And this our dispensation shall continue of force until the Grand Lodge shall grant a Warrant of Constitution for the same, or this dispensation be revoked by us or by the Grand Lodge aforesaid.

Given under our hand and the seal of the Grand Lodge, [L. S.] at the Grand East of ...., this ... day of ...., A∴ L∴ 58 ..

....,

Grand Secretary.

....,

Grand Master.

III. CHARTER OR WARRANT OF CONSTITUTION GRANTED BY THE GRAND LODGE.

WARRANT OF CONSTITUTION.

To all whom it may concern:

The Most Worshipful Grand Lodge of Ancient Freemasons of ...., in Grand Communication assembled, SEND GREETING:

Know ye, that we, the Grand Lodge of Ancient Freemasons of ...., have authorized and empowered, and do hereby authorize and empower, our trusty and well-beloved brethren, A. B., Worshipful Master; C. D., Senior Warden; and E. F., Junior Warden, to open and hold a Lodge designated as ..... Lodge, No...., under our register and jurisdiction, at ......, in the State of ......, or within three miles of the same.

And we do further authorize and empower the said brethren to Admit, Enter, Pass, and Raise Freemasons, according to the most ancient customs and usages of the craft, in all ages and nations throughout the world, and not otherwise.

And we do further authorize and empower the said brethren, and their successors in office, to hear and determine, all and singular, matters and things relative to the craft, within the jurisdiction of the said Lodge.

And lastly, we do hereby authorize, empower, and direct our said trusty and well-beloved brethren to install their successors in office, after being duly elected and chosen; to invest them with all the powers and dignities to their offices respectively belonging, and to deliver to them this WARRANT OF CONSTITU-TION; and such successors shall, in like manner, from time to time, install their successors, and proceed in the premises as above directed: such installation to be upon, or immediately preceding, the festival of St. John the Evangelist, during the continuance of the said Lodge forever.

Provided always, that the said above-named brethren and their successors do pay, and cause to be paid, due respect and strict obedience to the Most Worshipful Grand Lodge of An- cient Freemasons of .... aforesaid, and to the rules, regulations, and edicts thereof: otherwise, this Warrant of Constitution to be of no force nor virtue.

Given in open Grand Lodge, and under the hands of our Grand officers, and the seal of our Grand Lodge, at ..▲....., this .... day of ....., in the year of Light 58...

Q.... R....,   U.... V....,
Grand Master.   *Senior Grand Warden.*

S.... T....,   [L. S.]   W.... X....,
Deputy Grand Master.   *Junior Grand Warden.*

     Y.... Z...., *Grand Secretary.*

———

IV. PETITION FOR INITIATION.

To the Worshipful Master, Wardens and Members of ......
Lodge, No....

GENTLEMEN :

Being prompted by a favorable opinion conceived of the Institution, unbiased by the improper solicitation of friends and uninfluenced by mercenary motives, I voluntarily offer myself a candidate for the mysteries of Freemasonry to be conferred in your Lodge.

If elected, I promise cheerfully to conform to all the ancient usages and established customs of the fraternity.

I am by occupation a ...., aged .... years, and without any mental or physical defects which, as I am informed, would preclude my initiation.

I submit my character to your investigation, and ask your suffrages in my behalf.

I am, respectfully,

A...... B......

Recommended by

C...... D......, } Members of the
E..... F......, } Lodge.

V. PETITION FOR AFFILIATION.

To the Worshipful Master, Wardens and Brethren of ......
Lodge, No....

BRETHREN:

I fraternally apply for affiliation with your Lodge. I am a Master Mason in good standing, and with this petition submit my Demit from ..... Lodge, No..., of which Lodge I was last a member.

I am, fraternally,

G...... H .....

VI. MASTER MASON'S DIPLOMA OR CERTIFICATE,

COMMONLY CALLED A "GRAND LODGE CERTIFICATE."

To all Free and Accepted Masons throughout the globe—
Greeting.

Know ye, that our beloved Brother, ..., who has signed his name in the margin hereof, is a regular Master Mason of .... Lodge, No..., at ...., in the State of ...., and as such we desire and recommend that he be received and accepted by the Craft wheresoever dispersed over the face of the globe.

Given under our hands, and the s al of the Lodge, at ...., this .... day of ...., in the year of Light 587...

[L. s.] ...., *Worshipful Master.*
...., *Senior Warden.*
...., *Junior Warden.*
...., *Secretary.*

Grand Lodge of Ancient Free and Accepted Masons of ....

This is to certify that .... Lodge, No....., is a just and legally constituted Lodge working under the jurisdiction of the Grand Lodge of ...., and that this Diploma is entitled to full faith and credit among the brethren.

[L. s.] ....,
Grand Secretary.

VII. THE SAME DIPLOMA IN LATIN.

Omnibus Latomis per Orbem Terrarum Liberis Acceptisque.

S∴ S∴ S∴

Sciant omnes fratrem nostrum dilectissimum ...... qui hujusce in margine nomen suum ascripsit, post debitas constitutasque probationes, sublimem gradum MAGISTRI assecutum esse et in Collegium Latomorum vulgo appellatum ...... No... coöptatum esse.

Quamobrem eum singulis ejusdem gradus juribus ac privilegiis frui volumus.

In cujus rei testimonium, manus nostras et sigillum quo in hisce utimur apponi curavimus, ... die mensis ...... anno lucis 587...

...., *Magister.*

...., ..., *Custos Senior.*
Scriba. ...., *Custos Junior.*

VIII. APPLICATION FOR A DEMIT.

To the Worshipful Master, Wardens and Brethren of ......
Lodge, No....

BRETHREN:

Being desirous of severing my connection with ......, No...,
for the purpose of uniting with another, I fraternally apply for a
Demit. All dues to the Lodge have been paid.

Fraternally,

J...... K.......

IX. A DEMIT.

Lodge No. ...., under the jurisdiction of the Grand Lodge
of ......

To all whom it may concern— Greeting:

This is to certify that Brother ......, whose name appears
in the margin of this Demit, is a Master Mason in good standing, and clear of the books, and was a member of this Lodge,
and as such we recommend him to the fraternal regard of all
Free and Accepted Masons, wheresoever dispersed over the face
of the globe.

In testimony whereof, we have caused this Demit to be
[L. S.]   signed by the Worshipful Master and Secretary,
and the seal of the Lodge to be affixed, this ... day
of ...., A. L∴ L∴ 587....

...., *W. Master.*

...., *Secretary.*

X. LODGE SUMMONS

...... Lodge, No. ...

BROTHER:

You are hereby summoned to attend a ...... communication

of this Lodge, to be holden at .... o'clock on ..... evening
the .... day of ...... Herein fail not.

By order, A...... C......,

Secretary.

XI. NOTIFICATION FOR TRIAL.

...... Lodge, No....

BROTHER:

You are hereby notified that at a regular Communication of
...... Lodge, No..., holden on Thursday Evening, ... of
...... charges and specifications, a copy of which is hereunto
annexed, were preferred against you by Bro.·. ......

Whereupon it was ordered that the said charges and specifications be investigated at a trial to be holden in open Lodge, at
the next regular Communication, to be holden on Thursday,
the ... day of ......, of all which you will take due notice and
govern yourself accordingly.

By order of the Lodge,

A..... C.....,

Secretary.

XII. NOTICE OF EXPULSION, &c.

...... Lodge, No....

To R.·. W.·. Brother..., M. M.

Grand Secretary of the Grand Lodge of ......

R.·. W.·. Sir and Bro.·.

You are hereby notified that at a regular Communication of
...... Lodge, No..., holden on Thursday, the ... of ...., 1870,
Brother.........., after due trial, was expelled from all the
privileges of Masonry (or suspended, as the case may be), and it
was ordered that notice thereof be given to the Grand Lodge.

A...... C......,

Secretary.

V. FORM FOR KEEPING THE MINUTES OF A LODGE.

[The following form embraces the most important transactions that usually occur during the Communication of a Lodge, and it may therefore serve as an exemplar for the use of secretaries.]

' A regular Communication of..... Lodge, No..., was holden at......, on the .... day of...., 587...

PRESENT.

Bro. A. B...., W. Master,

" B. C...., S. Warden,

" C. D...., J. Warden,

" D. E...., Treasurer,

" E. F....., Secretary,

" F. G...., S. Deacon,

" G. H...., J. Deacon,

" H. I....,
" J. K...., } Stewards,

" K. L...., Tiler,

Members.

Bro. L. M....

M. N....

N. O....

O. P.....

Visitors.

Bro. P. Q....., Lodge No...

Q. R....., " No...

R. S....., " No...

The Lodge was opened in due form on the third degree of Masonry.

The minutes of the last regular Communication, and of a special Communication holden on ......, were read and confirmed.

The Committee on the petition of Mr. C. B....., a candidate for initiation, reported favorably, whereupon he was balloted for and duly elected.

The Committee on the petition of Mr. D. C...., a candidate for initiation, reported favorably, whereupon he was balloted for, and the box appearing foul, he was rejected.

The Committee on the petition of Mr. E. D....., a candidate for initiation, reported unfavorably, whereupon he was declared rejected without a ballot.

Brother S. R..... an Entered 'Apprentice, having applied for advancement, he was duly elected to take the second degree; and Brother W. Y....., a Fellow Craft, was, on his application for advancement, duly elected to take the third degree.

A petition for initiation from Mr. G. F..... enclosing the usual amount, and recommended by Bros. C. D..... and H. I....., was referred to a Committee of Investigation, consisting of Bros. G. H....., L. M....., and O. P.....

A letter was read from Mrs. T. V....., the widow of a Master Mason, when the sum of twenty dollars was voted for her relief.

The Amendment to Article 10, Section 5, of the By-Laws of this Lodge, proposed by Brother M. N..... at the Communication of..... .., was read a third time, adopted by a constitutional majority, and ordered to be sent to the Grand Lodge for approval and confirmation.

The Lodge of Master Masons was then closed, and a Lodge of Entered Apprentices opened in due form.

Mr. C. B...., a candidate for initiation, being in waiting, was duly prepared, brought forward and initiated as an Entered Apprentice, he paying the usual fee.

The Lodge of Entered Apprentices was then closed, and a Lodge of Fellow Crafts opened in due form.

Brother S. R...., an Entered Apprentice, being in waiting, was duly prepared, brought forward and passed to the degree of a Fellow Craft, he paying the usual fee.

The Lodge of Fellow Crafts was then closed, and a Lodge of Master Masons opened in due form.

Brother W. Y....., a Fellow Craft, being in waiting, was duly prepared, brought forward and raised to the sublime degree of a Master Mason, he paying the usual fee.

Amount received this evening as follows:

Petition of Mr. G. F........$5
Fee of Bro. C. B..........5
" " " S. R..........5
" " " W. Y..........5——Total, $20,

all of which was paid over to the Treasurer.

There being no further business, the Lodge was closed in due form and harmony.

E...... F......

Secretary.

[These minutes should be read at the close of the meeting, that the Brothers present may suggest any necessary alterations or correct omissions; and then at the beginning of the next regular Communication, that they may be confirmed. After which they should be transcribed from the rough Minute Book, in which they were first entered, into the permanent Record-Book of the Lodge.]

VI. FORM FOR BY-LAWS OF A LODGE.

[One of the greatest of the difficulties which are attendant on the organization of a new Lodge is the adoption of a suitable and efficient code of By-Laws for its government. This difficulty is often rendered still greater by the inexperience of its members, often young Masons, unacquainted with the usages of the craft and the prerogatives of a subordinate Lodge. The following model of a Code of By-Laws is therefore submitted, as in part tending to remove this difficulty. It is not to be expected that every section of this form will be always adopted. Local circumstances and special regulations of a Grand Lodge may render some of them unnecessary or inexpedient. Yet, the general form will not, it is believed, be found useless as a guide for the preparation of a proper code.]

ARTICLE 1.

Name, Officers, &c.

Section. 1. The name and title of this Lodge shall be......
Lodge, No....

Sec. 2. Its officers shall consist of a Worshipful Master, Senior and Junior Wardens, Treasurer, Secretary, Senior and Junior Deacons, two Stewards, and a Tiler.

Sec. 3. The first five officers shall be elected by ballot, and by a majority of the votes present, for twelve months, at the regular communication preceding the festival of St. John the Evangelist, and shall be installed on or before the said festival; on which festival they shall assume the duties and prerogatives of their respective offices. But every officer shall retain his office until his successor shall have been installed.

SEC. 4. On the night of installation, the Worshipful Master elect shall appoint the Senior Deacon and Tiler; the Senior Warden shall appoint the Junior Deacon, and the Junior Warden shall appoint the two Stewards.

SEC. 5. The Worshipful Master elect shall, on the night of election, appoint a Committee of three to examine the Treasurer and Secretary's books, which Committee shall report at the next regular Communication.

ARTICLE II.

Of the Worshipful Master.

SEC. 1. The Worshipful Master shall preside at all times when present. He shall have charge of the Warrant of Constitution, Jewels, and Furniture. He shall be empowered to convene the Lodge on any emergency which in his judgment shall require the same. He shall see that the rules and regulations of the Grand Lodge of........., as well as the By-Laws of this Lodge, be strictly obeyed; that his Officers perform their duties faithfully; that the Annual Returns be made, and dues punctually paid to the Grand Lodge. He shall appoint all Committees, and be *ex-officio* Chairman of the same, when he shall think proper to attend.

SEC. 2. On all questions where the votes of the Lodge are equally divided, the Master shall be entitled to the casting vote in addition to his vote as a member.

SEC. 3. There can be no appeal from the decision of the Master, except to the Grand Lodge.

ARTICLE IV.

Of the Wardens.

SEC. 1. It shall be the duty of the Wardens to assist the Worshipful Master in the government of the Lodge, and in his absence to preside according to seniority, unless through courtesy they relinquish the right of presiding to a Past Master present.

ARTICLE V.

Of the Treasurer.

SEC. 1. The Treasurer shall keep an exact account of all the Funds of the Lodge, and all scrip and certificates of Stock, and all titles of property belonging to the Lodge. He shall pay all orders signed by the Worshipful Master, and countersigned by the Secretary, and those drawn on him by the Committee of Charity; he shall report the state of the funds, and the members in arrears, at the regular meetings in June and December in each year. He shall submit his books to inspection whenever required by the Worshipful Master or the Lodge. He shall give a bond for the faithful performance of his duties in such sum as the Lodge may determine.

ARTICLE VI.

Of the Secretary.

SEC. 1. The Secretary shall issue all summonses for stated Communications three days previous; and for extra Communications, when required by the Presiding Officer, and deliver them to the Tiler. He shall keep a record of all the proceedings of the Lodge, which may be committed to writing; and insert the names of the members and visitors. He shall receive all moneys due to the Lodge, and forthwith pay them over to the Treasurer, taking his receipt for the same. He shall make out the Annual Return to the Grand Lodge, agreeably to the form prescribed, and transmit the same to the Grand Lodge, after it has been signed by the Presiding Officer. He shall have his Minutes copied into the journal and ready for examination at the regular Communication preceding the festival of St. John the Evangelist in each year.

ARTICLE VII.

Of the Deacons.

SEC. 1. The Senior and Junior Deacons shall perform all the duties appertaining to their respective offices according to Masonic usage under the direction of the Worshipful Master and Wardens.

ARTICLE VIII.

Of the Stewards.

SEC. 1. The Stewards shall, under the direction of the Junior Warden, prepare and superintend any banquet of the Lodge. They shall also be intrusted with the preparation of Candidates as the Assistants of the Senior Deacon, and with the Examination of visitors.

ARTICLE IX.

Of the Tiler.

SEC. 1. The Tiler must be a worthy Master Mason. It shall be his duty to serve all summonses and notifications delivered to him by the Secretary; to prepare the room for the Communications of the Lodge, and carefully to collect and replace the Jewels and Furniture after the Lodge is closed. For the faithful performance of his duties he shall receive the sum of......'ollars annually.

Of the Standing Committees.

Sec. 1. The Worshipful Master, Wardens, Treasurer, and Secretary shall be a Standing Committee on the Funds, whose duty it shall be to make sale or commutation of Stock, or other property of the Lodge, when so ordered by the Lodge. Also to invest such cash as may be, from time to time, in the hands of the Treasurer, and which they may be directed to invest by the Lodge.

Sec. 2. A Committee of Charity, to consist of three members, shall be annually appointed at the regular Communication in January, to whom may be referred all applications for relief during the recess of the Lodge. The majority of the Committee shall have power to draw on the Treasurer for a sum in each case not exceeding ..... dollars.

Of Initiation and Affiliation.

Sec. 1. Any person wishing to be initiated into the mysteries of Freemasonry in this Lodge, must apply by petition, at a regular Communication, recommended by two members, and enclosing not less than .... dollars, upon which a Committee of three shall be appointed to inquire into his qualifications, and to report at the next stated Communication.

SEC. 2. Should the report of the Committee be favorable, he may be balloted for, and if unanimously elected, he shall receive the degrees conferred by the Lodge, on his paying the fees established by the Grand Lodge. But should one dissenting ball appear, the ballot shall be repeated; and if one black ball shall then appear, the candidate shall be declared to be rejected, and the money enclosed in his letter shall be returned to him. But the rejected candidate may re-apply at any subsequent stated Communication of the Lodge, provided the same preliminary measures of a petition, recommendation, reference to a committee and ballot, are observed as in the previous application.

SEC. 3. The same principles and regulations as to petition, investigation, and unanimous ballot, shall govern the application of brethren for affiliation.

SEC. 4. Should any candidate neglect to attend for initiation within three stated Communications of his being duly notified of his election, the money enclosed in his letter shall be forfeited to the Lodge, and he shall not be admitted without a new ballot, unless a reasonable excuse is assigned.

ARTICLE XII.
Of Life and Honorary Members.

SEC. 1. Any member of this Lodge may become a life member upon paying such sum as may be determined by the Lodge, but no life member is exempt from being expelled, suspended, or subjected to other Masonic discipline, for cause shown.

ARTICLE XIII.
Of Demission.

SEC. 1. Any member of this Lodge, who is in good standing and not under charges, may be permitted to demit upon giving written notice of his intention to the Lodge, requesting the said demit, and paying up his arrears in full.

Of Trials.

SEC. 1. All charges must be made in writing, signed by the accuser, and read by him at a regular Communication of the Lodge. The accused shall then be furnished with an attested copy of the charges by the Secretary, and he shall, at the same time, be informed of the time and place appointed by the Lodge for the trial.

SEC. 2. If the accused is living beyond the jurisdiction of the Lodge, the charges shall be communicated to him by letter through the Post Office, and a reasonable time allowed for his answer before the Lodge proceeds to trial.

SEC. 3. The trial shall commence at a regular Communication of the Lodge, but may be continued at special Communications convened for that purpose.

SEC. 4. The Lodge shall be opened in the highest degree to which the accused has attained, and the examinations shall take place in the presence of the accuser and the accused, if they desire it; but the final decision shall always be made in the third degree.

SEC. 5. The evidence of profanes, or brethren of an inferior degree, must be taken by a committee, and reported to the Lodge. The accuser and the accused shall have a right to be present at such examinations.

SEC. 6. The testimony of Master Masons must be taken on their honor as Master Masons; that of others in such manner as shall be agreed on by the parties or determined by the Committee.

SEC. 7. When the testimony and arguments are concluded,

the accuser and the accused shall retire, ard the Worsl.ipful Master shall put the question of "guilty" or "not guilty" to the Lodge. The question shall be taken by ballot, a white ball denoting *not guilty*, and a black one *guilty*. If two-thirds of the balls are black, the accused shall be declared guilty. Every member present is bound to vote, unless excused by unanimous permission.

SEC. 8. If the verdict be guilty, the Worshipful Master shall then put the question as to punishment, beginning with expulsion, and going on, if necessary, to indefinite suspension, definite suspension, and public and private reprimand. For expulsion, or suspension, definite or indefinite, the votes must be two-thirds of those present, but for reprimand a majority will be sufficient. The votes on the nature of punishment must be taken by a show of hands.

SEC. 9. If the residence of the accused is not known, or if he refuses or neglects to attend, the Lodge may, nevertheless, proceed to the trial without his presence—a reasonable time, in the former case, being allowed for the necessary search for him.

ARTICLE XV.

Of Rules of Order.

SEC. 1 When the Presiding Officer takes the Chair, every officer and member shall immediately take his place, and observe strict order and decorum.

SEC. 2. No member shall speak until he first rise, and respectfully address the Presiding Officer; nor shall he speak more than twice on any subject, unless to explain, or by permission from the Chair.

SEC. 3. All questions of Order shall be decided by the Presiding Officer, without appeal to the Lodge.

Sec. 4. All questions before the Lodge, not otherwise partic ularly defined, shall be decided by a majority of the Lodge.

Sec. 5. No person shall be permitted to leave the room during the session of the Lodge but by permission of the Presiding Officer.

Sec. 6. No Officer shall leave his seat except it be in the discharge of his official duties.

Sec. 7. No Brother shall move from his place, nor shall any member or visitor be permitted to enter at any time during the opening or closing of the Lodge, the reading of the minutes, at the time of preparing a candidate, or while conferring a degree, unless with permission of the Chair.

Sec. 8. If any member or visitor shall be guilty of indecorum during the session of the Lodge, the Worshipful Master may, at his discretion, reprimand or exclude him, for that Communication, from the Lodge.

Sec. 9. No member of any Lodge, who is more than twelve months in arrears, shall be eligible to any office, or be allowed to vote at the election of Officers.

Sec. 10. The Constitution of the Grand Lodge, and the landmarks of the Order, shall be the governing principles of every Lodge, and shall be refer ed to in all cases of doubt. In all decisions of the Lodge, appeals may be made to the Grand Lodge; but until the opinion of the latter is made known, the decision of the former is held valid.

ARTICLE XVI.

Of Alterations of the By-Laws.

No additions, alterations, or amendments, can be made to the By-Laws of any Lodge, unless first presented, in writing, to the Chair, then read at three stated Communications, and approved of by three-fourths of the members present; nor can any of these By-Laws be suspended, even by unanimous consent.